Masterpieces of the
Museo Egizio
in Turin

OFFICIAL GUIDE
by *Eleni Vassilika*

FONDAZIONE
MUSEO DELLE
ANTICHITÀ
EGIZIE
DI TORINO

SCALA

The History of the Museo Egizio in Turin

Visitors to the Museo Egizio always marvel at the wealth of material on display (6,500 objects). The growth of the collections over years of excavations in Egypt (at a time when archaeological finds were divided up between Egypt and the institution doing the excavating) has resulted in a further 26,500 objects in storage. This catalogue only presents a small sample of the extraordinary collections of the Museo Egizio, the only museum completely dedicated to Egyptian art and culture outside of Egypt. Indeed, it is said to be the second most important museum of its kind after the one in Cairo.

The collections of the Museo Egizio have a long and illustrious history. The first object to come to Turin, a bronze altar table top (the *Mensa Isiaca*) acquired by King Charles Emanuel I in 1628, arrived with a number of other antiquities to be housed in the University of Turin in 1723. Eventually, King Charles Emanuel III commissioned the professor of botany Vitaliano Donati to go to Egypt and the Levant (1759-62) to acquire further antiquities. The crates of antiquities and botanical specimens arrived in Turin in 1763. Similar moves were made elsewhere during the 18th century: the French King Louis XIV also sent an agent to Egypt to collect manuscripts, coins and curios and to describe the contents of the pyramids, while the Danish King Christian VI sent Frederick Lewis Norden to record the monuments of Egypt in 1755.

It was Napoleon who was the key to bringing Egypt to the attention of the world. He went to Egypt in 1798, accompanied by 167 intellectuals known as 'savants'. Theirs was to be the first thorough exploration of Egypt. The savants recorded the monuments still standing, some of which have since disappeared, and they collected objects and samples of the flora and fauna. Among the objects found by Napoleon's soldiers was the now famous Rosetta Stone. On the defeat of the French experditionary force, all the antiquities that had been collected were handed over to the British under the terms of the Treaty of Alexandria (1801). Despite the loss of their finds, the French produced a series of magnificent large-format volumes (*Description de l'Ègypte*) documenting the massive Napoleonic expedition.

The Rosetta Stone confiscated from Napoleon by the British, and now in the British Museum, is a slab inscribed with a royal text in three scripts (hieroglyphs, demotic Egyptian and Greek). This provided the crucial clue to the decipherment of hieroglyphs. Ironically, it was the Frenchman Jean-François Champollion, and not a rival British colleague, who deciphered the royal names enclosed in 'cartouches', using the Greek text on the same slab as a reference (in 1822). Champollion himself would come to Turin two years later to study a newly arrived collection.

Napoleon's and Champollion's discoveries and the published reports of ancient Egypt sparked a mania for collecting in Europe.

Diplomats stationed in Egypt, such as the British consul Henry Salt, the Piedmontese Bernardino Drovetti who was appointed French consul, and the Damascus-born Armenian Giovanni Anastasi who served as the Swedish and Norwegian consul general, sold their finds and collections, not necessarily to the nation they represented, but to the highest bidder. For example, Salt sold his first collection to the British Museum (£2,000), his second collection to the King of France (£10,000) and his third collection at auction (£7,168). The British Museum, for its part, also bought from Anastasi and others.

It is in this context that Bernardino Drovetti from Turin, who had served as a colonel in Napoleon Bonaparte's Egyptian campaign, became the French Consul in Egypt, serving until 1814 and then again during the Restoration (1820-29). Drovetti assembled his first collection of 5,268 objects (statues, papyri, stelae, sarcophagi, mummies, bronzes, amulets and objects of everyday use), which he offered in turn to the Savoy king and to the Louvre, only to be refused. Eventually, Drovetti offered the collection to the Duke of Savoy, Charles Felix King of Sardinia, who acquired it for 400,000 lire on 24 January 1824.

The Drovetti Collection was sent by barge to Alexandria. Many of the statues were inscribed with Drovetti's name, presumably so that they would not be confused with the antiquities of other foreign consuls. Once the Savoy king had agreed to the purchase, everything was loaded onto seagoing vessels and brought to Livorno, where the collection was transferred onto ox-drawn artillery carts and carried overland to Turin. It is not clear how the objects were packed or whether they were all crated, because many shattered in transit and required conservation upon arrival. The sight of a colossal statue being transported through the countryside on an open cart would have filled onlookers with awe. The objects were deposited along with the other Egyptian antiquities already at the university, in the 17th century palace (built by the architect Guarino Guarini) that was used as an academy for the nobility. Champollion arrived in Turin as the Drovetti Collection was being unpacked, with the aim of studying the material and compiling a first catalogue of the Museum.

Other European cities were building Egyptian collections at around the same time. The Louvre acquired several private collections: Salt's second collection (1826), Drovetti's second collection (1827) and those of Clot-bey (1852), Anastasi (1857) and Tyskiewicz (1862). Berlin bought from Giuseppe Passalacqua (1828), Drovetti (his third collection 1836) and Saulnier (1839). Leiden received material from J.B. de Lescluze (1826/27), Salt and Anastasi (1828). Munich bought antiquities from Ferdinand Michel (1824) and Drovetti. After the first wave of collections assembled by consuls, private individuals entered the fray and began to collect antiquities that they sold to the newly created European museums.

While the new European museums were being set up, the Turin collection was finally opened to the public in 1831. The structure of the building did not allow the heavy statues carved from hard stone to be placed on the upper floors. So the statuary was relegated to two large galleries on the ground floor (the 'Statuario') completed in 1852. The collection grew with the transfer of 200 Egyptian objects to Turin from the Museo Kircheriano in Rome sometime around 1894.

The same year Ernesto Schiaparelli became Director of the Museo Egizio and went to Egypt to acquire further antiquities. Scholars had begun arriving in Egypt to excavate, and the legal system of *partage* allowed them to keep a portion of their finds. Thus, the newly created museums were able to enlarge their collections by means of further excavations. Schiaparelli began digging at several sites in Egypt in order to enrich the collections of the Museo Egizio in Turin. Among the places where he excavated were: Giza (1903), Ashmunein (1903-1904), Heliopolis (1903-1904), Qaw el-Kebir (1905-1906), Hammamiya (1905), the Valley of Queens at Thebes (1903-1906), Deir el-Medina (1905, 1909), Asyut (1905, 1908, 1910, 1911-1913), the Tomb of Kha at Thebes (1906), Gebelein (1910, 1911, 1914, 1920) and Aswan (1914). Between 1903 and 1920 some 18,000 objects excavated in twelve campaigns by Schiaparelli entered the Museo Egizio. Schiaparelli's later excavations (between 1911 and 1920) were conducted in collaboration with the anthropologist Giovanni Marro and with Giulio Farina, whose work at Gebelein (1930, 1935, 1937) brought further finds to the Museum.

During World War II, the Museo Egizio was obliged to close its doors to the public in 1942. The collections were packed up and moved to the basement. Following the increase in bombing activity, however, the collections were moved with the aid of the Wehrmacht to the castle at Agliè. In 1945 it was the Allied forces that transferred the antiquities back to Turin from Agliè so that the Museum could be opened again to the public the following year.

The Italian state allowed the creation of a public-private foundation which was given responsibility for the management of the collections of the Museo Egizio (on 19 December 2005), for a period of thirty years in the first instance. This is the first time an Italian state museum has been privatised and its progress and success are being observed as others follow suit. Thus the Museo Egizio found itself at the forefront of a great new experiment on the eve of the Winter Olympics in Turin. The Museum rose to the occasion and kicked off with a dramatic illumination of the 'Statuario' by the Oscar-winning art director Dante Ferretti. The Museum is now planning to double the space it occupies in the palace in order to enable it to display more of the material which deserves attention, but has hitherto lain in storage. Jean-François Champollion's apt words "the road to Memphis and Thebes passes through Turin" will continue to resonate for many years to come.

Eleni Vassilika
Director of the Fondazione Museo delle Antichità Egizie di Torino

EARLY FEMALE FIGURE

Painted terracotta
Dimensions: 25 x 17 x 11 cm
Predynastic Period, Naqada I (?)
(about 3700 BC)
Provenance unknown, acquired by
Schiaparelli in Egypt, 1900-1901
Inv. no. S. 1146

Early man's preoccupation was with creating objects that served his needs. Moulding a figure of a woman served a serious purpose. This figure, which is abbreviated with a thumb-like projection for a head and stumps for arms, is nevertheless ladylike in its pinched waist and large thighs. It is the lower part of the body in particular that is suggestive and indicates the purpose of such figures. Swollen hips, technically known as 'steatopygia', allude to a woman's procreative power. Indeed, even today, this attribute is often attractive to the opposite sex. The figure may represent a woman or a deity, but in any case, it was probably intended to ensure fertility by magic. The angle of the thighs, relative to the trunk of the body, may also suggest a squatting position for giving birth. The head has been pinched into shape and has been decorated with sweeping black eyes outlined in malachite. Fish are painted in black on her chest, and there are zigzag patterns at the hips that may depict tattoos or actual bead and shell girdles. Further animal motifs appear on her back.

The first human figures come from the earliest phases of the Predynastic culture (called Faiyum A). In the subsequent Badarian culture, the mostly female figures were modelled in terracotta or ivory, and were characterised by a dominant pubic triangle. Later, in the Naqada Period, the human figures could have additional painted details, as they do here.

PREHISTORIC BURIAL

Mummy (S. 293), *leather bags* (S. 282,
S. 295), *throw stick* (S. 292) *and arrows*
(S. 298), *reed sandals* (S. 294) *and baskets*
(S. 301-303)
Predynastic Period, Naqada I (?) (about 3700 BC)
Provenance unknown, acquired by
Schiaparelli in Egypt, 1900-1901

This group of objects has been recomposed
from the contents of a number of graves
from the predynastic (or prehistoric) period.
Nevertheless, the cohesiveness of the group
is attested by a number of excavated graves.
For example, there is a naturally mummified
corpse with funerary equipment in the
British Museum. The body here is that of
a man who has been mummified naturally.
Burial in a shallow grave has allowed the
dry warmth of the desert to desiccate and
naturally mummify the body. Observation
of this process probably led the Egyptians
to develop a more reliable mummification
process. Here much of the skin of the head
and hands is missing, though in other areas
traces of fabric are still attached to the skin.
Consistently, the deceased was laid in a foetal
position, lying on the left side with the head
pointing south, and thus facing the setting
sun. The fact that the body is in a foetal
position may suggest not only the wish for
rebirth, but also the idea that death was
considered a transitory state of sleep before
reaching the Afterlife. Military weapons and
personal effects were normally included in
such early male burials, in some cases with
sandals and baskets of food as well. The
objects included in graves of this early date
would have been the personal effects of the
deceased, the things that he or she would
have required in the Afterlife.

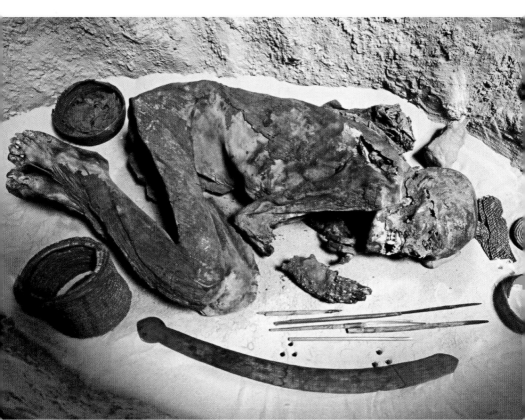

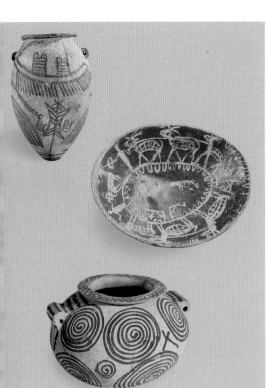

COLLECTION OF PREDYNASTIC POTTERY

Black-topped vase (S. 477)
Dimensions: 14,1 x 8,3 cm

White painted bowl (S. 1827)
Dimensions: 4,4 x 17,1 x 14 cm
Naqada I (about 3700 BC)

Red painted buff vase (S. 413)
Dimensions: 15 x 10,4 cm

Globular vase (Provv. 653)
Dimensions: 16 x 23 cm
Naqada II (about 3500 BC)

Provenance unknown, acquired by
Schiaparelli in Egypt, 1900-1901
Inv. nos. S. 477, S. 1827, S. 413, Provv. 653

Pottery is the measure of any early culture.
Construction was done by hand, before
the introduction of the potter's wheel.
These vessels from the Predynastic Period
(especially the so-called Naqada I) are
known as 'black-topped ware', due to the
fact that their surfaces, usually covered
with red slip, were blackened around the
rim. This dichromatic effect was obtained

during the firing in primitive kilns when
the vases were turned upside down.

Other decorated types of vessels in this
period were covered with red slip that was
then painted with simple off-white stick
figures of animals and humans (usually
hunters). In the next phase, Naqada II, the
centre for the production of vessels moved to
a new location where the clay was altogether
different. The vessels had a buff fabric,
which was not covered with a red slip. The
potters painted with red (instead of creamy
white) pigment, directly onto the buff
surface. The subjects were more developed
than in the earlier period, with images of
many-oared ships, more substantial male
and female figures and animals. Some of the
vessels were painted with geometric patterns
to imitate basketry or with spirals to imitate
the inclusions in actual stone vessels, which
were, of course, more expensive to produce.
In any case, both pottery and stone versions
have similar shapes. During the pre-dynastic
period, when Egypt was theoretically not
yet unified, pottery was produced in certain
centres and then disseminated throughout
Egypt. This diffusion indicates organised
trade and reveals social cohesion and unity of
purpose.

PAINTED LINEN

Linen (*Linus usitatissimum*)
Dimensions: ca. 390 x 95 cm
Predynastic Period, Naqada II
(about 3500 BC)
Provenance: Farina excavations, Gebelein,
1930
Inv. no. S. 17138

These are the earliest painted textiles
known, found in Gebelein in a Predynastic
burial at the side of a corpse. The painted
images on the now fragmentary linen are
related to the contemporary decoration
on Naqada II pottery. Many-oared ships
(the oars bent at an angle as if seen
through the water) with a cabin on deck,
with oarsmen in silhouette are depicted.
Other fragments show female figures
dancing or standing before a man who is
spearing a hippopotamus. This particular
scene may be an apotropaic one that was
intended magically to prevent the animal
from attacking boatmen. These Nilotic
scenes have a long tradition in Egyptian
art, well into the Roman Period. Not far
from this tomb, one with plaster walls at
Hierakonpolis was painted in a similar way
(it is now in the Cairo Museum). Egyptian
art does not exist in a void, and therefore
one expects to find similar iconography
on various supports, such as textiles,
decorated walls and pottery, all from the
Naqada II Period. It is possible that this
textile once hung on a wall so that the
various scenes could be read. The fringed
remnants along the border suggest that it
was indeed a decorative 'canvas'.

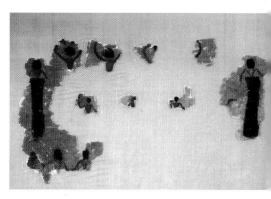

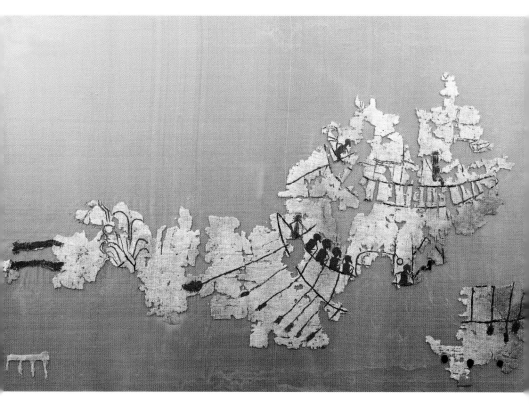

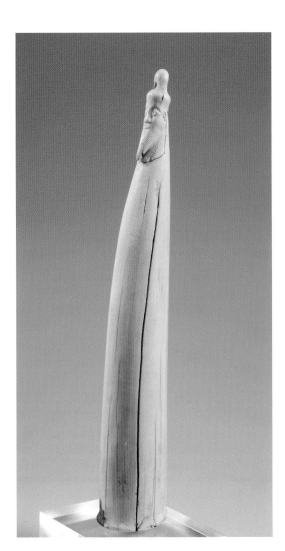

TUSK CARVED IN THE FORM OF A BEARDED MAN

Ivory
Dimensions: 23,8 x 4 cm
Predynastic Period, Naqada II (?)
(about 3500 BC)
Provenance unknown, acquired by
Schiaparelli in Egypt, 1900-1901
Inv. no. S. 1068

As they were adapted to the shape of the tusk, carved ivory figures were usually shown standing, rarely seated. In this case a craftsman of the fourth millennium BC has transformed the tip of the hippopotamus tusk into the head of a bearded man wearing a box-like headdress surmounted by a projection with a hole in it. Could this be a crown? It has an uncanny resemblance to the so-called red crown of Lower Egypt, worn by the king after the unification of Egypt. However, the base of the tusk terminates in an everted lip, which suggests a long robe-like garment. The fact that the figure is pierced so that it can be hung on a string indicates that it is the image of a person or deity of some importance to be worn around the neck of someone of less importance. This figure was created prior to the dynastic period, but the unification of Egypt was a process that took many forms and many centuries. A society with some degree of cohesion must have existed before the pharaonic period, as is evident from the production and distribution of pottery for example.

STATUE OF REDIT

Basalt
Dimensions: 82 x 32 x 43 cm
Old Kingdom, Dynasty III (2687-2632 BC)
Provenance: possibly from Saqqara, later
Drovetti Collection, 1824
Inv. no. C. 3065

In the Old Kingdom, statues of individuals
were placed in tombs. This figure dates
from the earliest period of unification, the
so-called 'Archaic Period', before the first
pyramids were built. The sculpture is of
a seated princess, whose name 'Redit, the
King's Daughter', appears in raised relief
on the base. She wears a long, heavy plaited
wig that is divided into three lappets on
either side of her head and on her back.
She is cubic in form with a short neck and
block-like body, but with thin arms, and
appears as if she is barely emerging from the
original block of stone. Although battered,
Redit's eyes are little more than buttonhole
openings. Later sculptors would develop an
elegant style for the eyes, adding rims that
terminate in long cosmetic stripes. Here
the large wig (ladies of rank wore wigs and
not their natural hair) is plaited in detail. It
is possible that the wig served as a support
to avoid breakage in a material that was
expensive to quarry and labour-intensive to
carve. Generally, a back pillar would serve
this purpose.
It is surprising to find a sculpture of such size
in a hard stone at such an early date. One
must recall that metal tools hard enough
to work basalt did not exist at this time, so
the artisan could only use stone tools harder
than the stone of the sculpture itself. A
female sculpture of this size and hardness is
extremely rare for this early date. The figure
was intended to double for the deceased, and
be animated by her *ka*-spirit.

INLAID COFFER

Wood, faience and ivory
Dimensions: 19 x 38 x 23 cm
Old Kingdom, Dynasty IV (2632-2510 BC)
Provenance: Schiaparelli excavations,
Gebelein, 1914
Inv. no. S. 15709

It is natural in all societies to want to
protect linen from dust. So it was in an
Old Kingdom tomb at Gebelein that the
linen was packed into this fine coffer.
The luxurious coffer is decorated with
inlaid tiles of ivory (usually derived from
hippopotamus tusks), and a kind of early
glass called faience (made of quartz fused
with a vitreous alkaline glaze coloured with
a copper compound). Here the faience
tiles are coloured dark and pale blue for
an alternating effect. These glassy colours
were the only ones that were available at
this date. It would be almost a thousand
years before a wider range of colours came
into use in faience production.

The coffer is designed to imitate natural
plant forms, also used in buildings. The
ivory panels along the sides are carved to
resemble palm reeds, just like the walls
of simple buildings. The faience band
below the lid may reflect how these reed
mats were tied at the top of the walls with
leather straps. The lid of the coffer is richly
decorated with lotus blossoms against an
ivory field and separated by vertical bands
of blue faience. The fact that the lotus
often appeared in architecture as a column
may here reflect a wonderful columned
hall. The coffer is fitted with wooden legs
that may have protected it against vermin.
The inside of the coffer was painted red.

FALSE DOOR OF UHEM-NEFERET

Limestone
Dimensions: 202,5 x 170 x 37 cm
Old Kingdom, Dynasty IV (2632-2510 BC)
Provenance: Schiaparelli excavations, Giza,
1903
Inv. no. S. 1840

A false door is a series of door jambs and
architraves sculpted into a tomb wall as a
means of allowing the deceased to come
and go. It was also the point where the
living could leave food offerings for the
nourishment of the deceased. Thus it was
the point of contact between the living and
the dead. This door has been carved in raised
relief so that the figures and hieroglyphic
texts stand out from the background. The
door comes from the tomb of a woman
named Uhem-neferet, who is depicted on
the central block that sits on the double
architrave. Uhem-neferet is shown seated
before a single-pedestal table covered with
tall and thin loaves of bread. Hieroglyphs

identify the rest of the food offerings. The texts on the architrave give her titles as the 'Beloved Daughter of the King, privileged before her mother, Uhem-neferet'. Her high rank explains why Uhem-neferet was one of the few women of the period who had a tomb of her own and was not dependent on that of a spouse. The door jambs depict figures, including her offspring (note the naked boy on the right) delivering baskets of food, linens and sandals as part of the funerary rites.

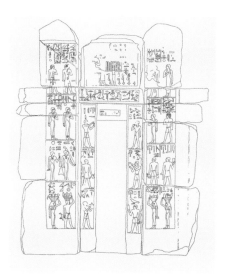

ITETI'S BURIAL

Head of Iteti (S. 1876)
Limestone
Dimensions: 26 x 22 x 22 cm

Two blocks (S. 1851, S. 1852)
Painted limestone
Dimensions: 72 x 106 cm

Old Kingdom, Dynasty IV (2632-2510 BC)
Provenance: Schiaparelli excavations,
Giza, 1903
Inv. nos. S. 1876, S. 1851, S. 1852

Iteti was the 'Chief of the Priests of the
Pyramid of [King] Khephren', the builder
of the second great pyramid at Giza.
Iteti's tomb originally consisted of two
underground chambers, located in the
eastern cemetery for courtiers near the
earlier pyramid of Khufu. At some later
point two more chambers were added, as
well as a large mud brick superstructure.

This building was, like others of the
period, bench-like in shape and therefore
in modern studies, given the Arabic
name 'mastaba'. Set into the walls of this
superstructure were large limestone blocks
painted with distinctive and anatomically
detailed fowls in a series, almost as if for a
zoological publication.

The sculpted figure of Iteti was originally
placed in a small chamber (Arabic: serdab)
within the superstructure. All that survives
is the head and lower body of the seated
sculpture. Iteti's head is carved in the
style of the period. He wears a shoulder-
length wig made up of rows of tightly
stepped curls. The statue was vandalised
in antiquity and the eyes, sometimes with
copper rims once inlaid in other materials
(usually black-and-white stone), were
gouged out by tomb robbers. An unusual
feature of the sculpture is the low-relief
moustache that was probably painted
in antiquity. Indeed most statues carved

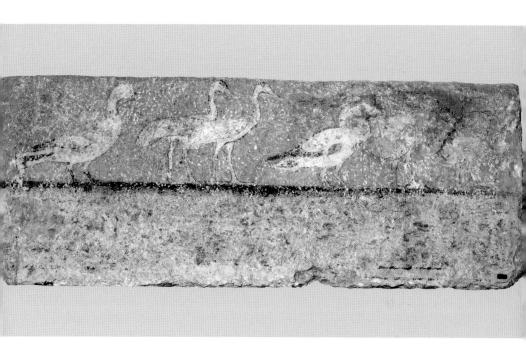

from stone, especially from pale stone, were painted in ancient Egypt. The lower part of the figure is carved as if seated with its hands resting on its lap, the right one in a fist and the left one with the palm flat against the thigh, according to the convention of the period. The stool on which Iteti sits is articulated with leonine legs.

OLD KINGDOM MUMMY OF AN UNKNOWN MAN FROM AN UNPLUNDERED TOMB

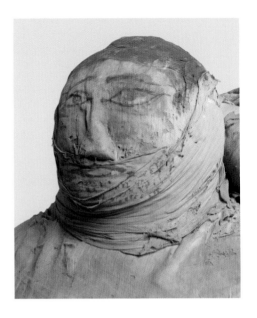

Human remains wrapped in linen
Dimensions: 163 x 55 x 30 cm
Old Kingdom, Dynasty V (about 2450 BC)
Provenance: Schiaparelli excavations, Gebelein, 1911
Inv. no. S. 13966

The director of the Museo Egizio, Ernesto Schiaparelli, and Virginio Rosa were certainly excited when they and their team discovered the entrance to an as yet unopened tomb at Gebelein on 28 January 1911. The rock-cut tomb had three chambers, but one was empty, while another housed a wooden coffin and some offerings (the planks used for lifting and transporting it along with the ropes were left *in situ*) and the largest of the chambers held three coffins (one of stone) along with a great multitude of objects.

The earliest mummified corpses in the Museo Egizio come from this tomb. The best-preserved mummy (158 cm tall) was located inside a stone coffin in the largest room. The limbs were wrapped separately and the bandages over the face were painted with facial features and hair in black pigment. Nipples too were indicated on the chest wrappings.
This tomb, which dates from the Fifth Dynasty, when pyramids were still being built, was well equipped with much of what was necessary in life. Loaves of bread, more than 30 large and small vessels (as magical models) and plates and bowls were found in the room around the coffins. The mummies were cushioned by long lengths of linen, and some rolls of which were left behind, stored in coffers. Especially beautiful carved wooden headrests were placed in the tomb. The Egyptians normally slept on their side with the neck resting on a crescent-shaped support that stood on a central pedestal. Although this may seem uncomfortable to the modern observer, it was often cushioned with fabric. Even the deceased's sandals were nearby. In short, all sorts of objects of everyday use were included in the tomb, presumably in order to equip the dead for the Afterlife. Mention has been made of the small model vessels, which had a magical function. Likewise, the miniature oared boats, the principal means of transport in this period, that were included in this multiple burial.

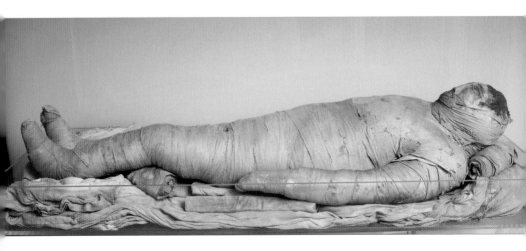

THE YOUNG MAN MEMI

Wood
Dimensions: 47,5 x 10,5 x 22 cm
Old Kingdom, Dynasty VI, reign of Pepi II
(about 2300 BC)
Provenance: possibly Saqqara, acquired by
Schiaparelli in Egypt, 1900-1901
Inv. no. S. 1197

Although royal statuary was normally carved from durable stone, there was a substantial production of wooden statues, especially for private individuals. The advantage of wood over stone was that it was closer to hand and did not require quarrymen and transport, and was more easily worked. A wooden figure could be assembled from parts dowelled together, and could be shown striding easily into the third dimension without the support of a back pillar or a filler between the legs or arms and torso, as was employed in stone sculptures.

The naked figure of Memi, whose name appears on the base, is carved with the freedom that comes with the material. His body and legs were sculpted from a single piece of wood, the arms were separately dowelled and the whole was slotted into the base, on which the feet were already carved. The dowel for the right arm, which is missing, is still visible. Memi wears his hair short-cropped and displays the nondescript ideal features of the late Old Kingdom. His nudity may be due to his youth, since children were normally shown naked, but with a finger raised to the mouth. In this case the lack of the right hand does not help us. On the other hand, the figure may have had a length of fabric wrapped around the waist, as has been found elsewhere, and therefore represent a fully grown man.

THE INTACT TOMB OF INI

Figure (S. 13269)
Dimensions: 70 x 13 x 50 cm

Coffin (S. 13268/01)
Dimensions: 67 x 225 x 62 cm

Painted wood
First Intermediate Period (about 2100 BC)
Provenance: Schiaparelli excavations,
Gebelein, 1911
Inv. nos. S. 13268-13318

The intact tomb of Ini from the northern
necropolis at Gebelein was discovered by
Schiaparelli in 1911, and is reconstructed

here as it was found. The wooden
sarcophagus gives Ini's titles as Sole
Companion to the King, Treasurer, Head
of the Province, and Supervisor of the
Priests of the God Sobek. His sarcophagus
is a simple rectangular wooden coffin with
wedjat-eyes painted on the exterior, level
with the deceased's face and intended to let
him 'see' the offerings outside the coffin.
A small wooden figure of the deceased
himself, wearing a long wrap-around kilt
and gripping a staff (suggesting a high rank),
stood in the tomb. The figure of Ini was
meant to substitute for the body in case it
was destroyed.

The well-furnished tomb included plates

and vessels, small rope-woven bags for wheat and two 'dioramas' of a wooden granary and a bakery (to nourish the deceased). Also included are two model boats. Perhaps these were intended to transport Ini to visit Osiris, the King of the Netherworld, at Abydos. Whereas during the Old Kingdom the inner walls of the tombs were usually decorated (carved or simply painted) with various scenes of different activities, this is rare in the First Intermediate Period. In this later period, however, the registers of scenes of offerings and agricultural activities were telescoped into a series of miniature models. In this funerary context, the servants and workers depicted engaging

in food production in small wooden dioramas were meant to take the place of large-scale, expensive and labour-intensive wall decorations. The head and skin of an ox were also found in the tomb, but these features were a Nubian import rather than an Egyptian tradition.

WALL PAINTINGS FROM THE TOMB OF ITI

Slaughter of a black and white cow
(S. 14354/8)
Dimensions: 130 x 85 cm

Scene with silos (S. 14354/15)
Dimensions: 127 x 209 cm

Scene with boat (S. 14354/7)
Dimensions: 118 x 182 cm

Stuccoed and painted mud brick
First Instermediate Period, Dynasty VII-XI

(2190-1976 BC)
Provenance: Schiaparelli excavations, Gebelein, 1911
Inv. nos. S. 14354/8, S. 14354/15, S. 14354/7

Iti was the King's Chancellor and Commander of Troops. His burial was at Gebelein in a half rock-cut tomb (*saff*), unlike earlier high officials of the Old Kingdom whose tombs were granted by the their king and located in cemeteries near the king's burial. Iti lived at a time when rigid central authority had broken down, in the so-called First Intermediate Period that separates the Old Kingdom from the

Middle Kingdom. It was a time when power was shifting to the petty governors, whose towns, often on caravan crossroads, were strategically positioned in terms of trade. These 'nomarchs' (the word is derived from the Greek) grew in power in inverse proportion to the weakening of central authority. Their wealth enabled them to create their own monuments independent of those of the king.

In general, during the Old Kingdom, the limestone tomb walls were carved in raised relief, and subsequently, for the sake of economy, in sunk relief. At Gebelein,

however, the uneven quality of the stone made it necessary to cover the walls with a layer of mud mixed with organic material and then with a layer of plaster that was painted. These paintings were removed from the wall by poulticing, and sent to the Museum.

The large-format paintings from this tomb depict a number of remarkable scenes from daily life, in addition to the delivery of funerary offerings. The slaughter of a black-and-white cow was intended to present a picture of Iti's staff at work, but also magically to provide provisions for

him and his wife Neferu. One scene that takes place on two and a half registers depicts men delivering grain to dome-like granaries. Antelope, whose colours show them to be of different breeds, are depicted grazing in the half registers, below the silos. Famously in this scene, and in others, a donkey is shown with two saddlebags, but for reasons of perspective, the bag on the invisible far side of the donkey is rotated 180° to the frontal plane, so that it can be seen. This peculiar perspective is mentioned in numerous studies of Egyptian art. Iti evidently also commanded a large boat

with a cabin on which the cowhide shields are hung. In this period of uncertainty, it seems that it was necessary for Iti's men to be prepared for sniping from the banks. In this scene a helmsman at the rudder and sitting on the cabin above, gives instructions with an arm extended, as the crew prepare the sails and tie the ropes at the foot of the mast. The boat is about to sail south on some sort of expedition.

TWO RELIEFS FROM THE TOMB OF ITI

Iti and Neferu and Iti's brother (S. 13114)
Dimensions: 42 x 69 cm

Meeting with mercenaries (S. 13115)
Dimensions: 34 x 54 cm

Painted limestone
First Intermediate Period, Dynasty VII-XI
(2190-1976 BC)
Provenance: Schiaparelli excavations,
Gebelein, 1911
Inv. nos. S. 13114 , S. 13115

During the excavation of Iti's tomb, two
rectangular limestone stelae were also
brought to light. One stele is clearly funerary
in character. Carved in sunk relief, the
deceased Iti and his wife Neferu stand on
the 'divine' left side of the block. Iti's brother
stands to the right, facing the couple, and
extends his arms. He is probably officiating
at the funeral rites. The figures are joined
by two pet dogs at their feet. Behind Iti's
brother is a low table piled high with vessels
and the heads of ducks, antelope and a
cow. Small offering bearers (battered) with
carrying poles and food, followed by a man
and woman, possibly the children of the
deceased, reinforce the idea of offerings,
shown as they are on a secondary baseline
above. The block is bordered by a prayer
ending with an invocation to the living
to provide sustenance for the Afterlife.

Stylistically it is evident that the contours are clumsy and uneven. Note, for example the profile of Neferu with her arm and perfunctory hand overlapping the waist of her husband. An angle defines the base of her buttocks and the hem of her dress is undefined between the legs. The striations of the male kilts are uneven. The whole scene has a Picassoesque quality that compares poorly with the relief of the Old Kingdom.

On another block of sunk relief from the same tomb, two pairs of light- and dark-skinned men, armed with bows, are shown meeting. It is not clear whether one of these men is Iti himself. However, the fact that the men are of distinctively different skin tones implies that they are of different races, and may be mercenaries. Perhaps the darker men are the famous Nubian archers. The presence of this block in his tomb suggests that Iti regularly made military expeditions with mercenaries.

SARCOPHAGUS OF IQER

Wood, red and black ink
Dimensions: max. length 2 m
Date disputed, probably early Middle
Kingdom, Dynasty XI (2110-1976 BC)
Provenance: Schiaparelli excavations,
Gebelein, 1911
Inv. no. S. 15774

Just as small wooden 'dioramas' were
invented as a way of making tombs
inexpensively, so the sarcophagus became
a support for prayers and images that in
earlier, more affluent, times would have
been located on the tomb walls. This Middle
Kingdom coffin from Gebelein, whose date
is debated, is one such coffin, with friezes
depicting individual objects that were
supposed to accompany the deceased into
the Afterlife and columns of hieroglyphic
texts, side by side with scenes of the owner's
funeral. The stick-like figures are drawn in
red and black ink and the friezes range in
size. Uniquely, this coffin includes a map
of the land of the dead depicted with three
doors. The text specifies that only the central
door should be used.

The lid of the coffin functioned as a sort of
Egyptian star clock, on which the calendar
year was based. The rising of the stars, or the
configurations known as decans, are shown
in red on a kind of spread sheet, with the
name of each written in black in the cell
alongside. The Egyptian calendar consisted
of twelve months, composed of three ten-
day weeks, and including five extra days
(epagomenal) totalling 365 days and thus
eventually required adjustment. The year
had three seasons, made up of four months
each. There are only a small number of
coffin lids with such astronomical texts, that
ultimately functioned as a cosmic clock for
the deceased.

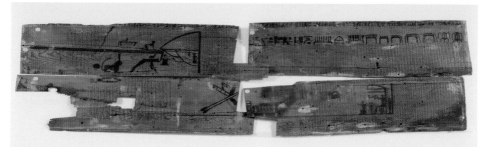

STELE OF MERU

Limestone
Dimensions: 172 x 70 x 13 cm
Early Middle Kingdom, Dynasty XI, reign of
Nebhepetre Mentuhotep II (about 2000 BC)
Provenance: probably Thebes, acquired by
the Museum before 1888 (possibly Drovetti
Collection, 1824)
Inv. no. C. 1447

Following the confusion of the First
Intermediate Period, there was a period of
consolidation before the Middle Kingdom
was fully established with its capital at
Thebes (modern Luxor). The large private

stele of Meru represents an historical
document of this moment. Meru was
Overseer of the Treasury, and thus the holder
of the state's purse strings. He commissioned
this magnificent funerary stele for himself
in a combination of raised and sunk relief.
The stele is divided essentially into two
sections, the lower one composed of three
registers. All the figures are in raised relief,
whereas the main body of the text in the
upper part is in sunk relief which was less
labour-intensive. There is no evidence here
of the clumsy draughtsmanship typical of the
First Intermediate Period. This stele reflects
a return to the high degree of skill typical
of the royal workshops that existed in the

Old Kingdom, though the style is not the same. The stele demonstrates that the Old Kingdom skills were not lost during the First Intermediate Period.

The crescent-shaped upper part of the stele gives Meru's titles and the date, year 46 of the reign of King Nebhepetre Mentuhotep II. The text begins with a funerary offering and an appeal to the living to remember Meru's name. This is an important aspect, because it demonstrates that the living without an offering in hand could be useful in guaranteeing the deceased's life, simply by repeating his (or her) name. Below, roughly in the centre of the stele, Meru stands on

the right and adores his father and another man on the left 'divine' side of the stele. In the register below, on a smaller scale, Meru appears with his mother at his side at an offering table piled high with food, including a leg of beef and a goose. A series of offering bearers with more food and tomb furnishings appear in even smaller scale on the bottom register.

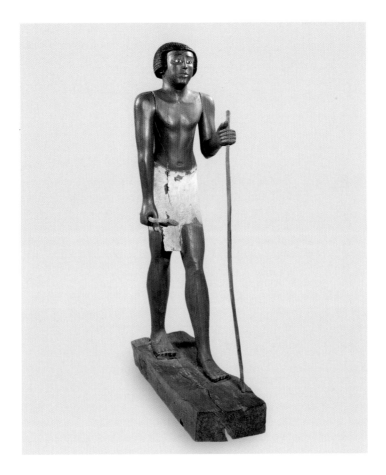

THE NOBLEMAN SHEMES

Wood
Dimensions: 123 x 32 x 73 cm
Middle Kingdom, Dynasty XI - early
Dynasty XII (about 2050-1947 BC)
Provenance: Schiaparelli excavations, Asyut,
1908
Inv. no. S. 8653

Local Egyptian timber was often poor in quality, so that fine timber was a luxury, normally imported from Lebanon. Stone was certainly more durable than wood, but it was harder to work and it inhibited the creation of larger sculptures for private individuals. It must be recalled that well into the Middle Kingdom, sculptures of private individuals were set up in tombs and not dedicated in temples. During the First Intermediate Period, when central authority had broken down, the provincial governors, often stationed near trade and caravan crossroads, became more powerful and were keen to imitate the pharaohs.

Shemes was one such nobleman whose tomb at Asyut included a wooden coffin decorated with *wedjat*-eyes. There were two wooden figures depicting him in the tomb; a smaller statuette and a larger one with eyes inlaid in coloured stone with bronze rims and cosmetic stripes. (The smaller statuette was more simply made, with only painted facial features.) His large figure, head, trunk and legs were carved from a single piece of fine hard timber. The arms, feet and base were carved separately and attached by means of tenons. Shemes holds a long staff in his raised left hand, and a small sceptre was inserted in his lowered right hand. These features, together with the forward-striding left leg, create an effect of great liveliness and movement. Shemes wears a wig, which is different in shape from that of the Old Kingdom, cut off at the ears. His face is longer and thinner than earlier figures and his eyebrows are high on the face, ignoring the contour of the eyes. Shemes is dressed in the tripartite *shendyt*-kilt, worn only by kings in the Old Kingdom. This fact represents a usurpation of a royal prerogative by a private individual.

MODEL BOAT

Wood
Dimensions: 50 x 15 x 87 cm
Middle Kingdom, Dynasty XI - early
Dynasty XII (about 2050-1947 BC)
Provenance: Tomb of Shemes, Schiaparelli
excavations, Asyut, 1908
Inv. no. S. 8657

As Egypt's prosperity depended on a narrow strip of fertile land either side of the river, it is obvious that the most important mode of travel and transport was the boat. The horse was introduced late, and then only sparingly, during the Second Intermediate Period following the Middle Kingdom. Thus, the Egyptians applied the idea of boat travel to everything. They imagined that even the sun traversed the sky in a boat. Two types of model boats were placed in Middle Kingdom tombs: papyrus skiffs, used by simple folk, and boats with ceremonial hulls. The boat was meant to transport the deceased magically to Abydos, the land of Osiris (god of the Netherworld). Shown with dismantled rigging on deck, meant the boat was travelling north (following the

south to north current of the Nile). When shown with upright mast and sails, the boat represented the southward journey (against the current). This boat, from the tomb of Shemes at Asyut, north of Abydos, would have been sailing against the current and relying on its sails. On the model, three sailors stand at the mast (now lost) in the act of raising the sails. Two figures, possibly representing the deceased in the company of a priest or his son acting as priest, are seated on deck under a canopy. A helmsman is seated behind them. A crew of sailors stand at the bow. All the sailors are red-skinned and wear the 'boatman's circlet' to hold their hair in place. The white rectangles on the deck are intended to imitate the movable planking. A large *wedjat*-eye is painted on the side of the boat as a protective amulet. A flotilla of three boats was found in the tomb of Shemes.

MIDDLE KINGDOM DIORAMAS

Wooden bakery (S. 8789)
Dimensions: 30 x 51 x 27 cm
Provenance: Asyut / Tomb of Kemhotep

Wooden granary (S. 8651)
Dimensions: 35 x 40 x 42 cm
Provenance: Asyut / Tomb of Kemhotep

Combined wooden bakery and brewery
(S. 8652)
Dimensions: 27 x 53 x 46 cm
Provenance: Asyut

Terracotta 'soul house' (S. 16030)
Dimensions: 18 x 31 x 40 cm
Provenance: Gebelein

Middle Kingdom, Dynasty XI - early
Dynasty XII (about 2050-1947 BC)

Inv. nos. S. 8789, S. 8651, S. 8652, S. 16030

To decorate the hewn stone walls of a
tomb was not within the reach of men and
women who did not enjoy royal patronage.
Perhaps as a way of economizing, a new
device was created in the First Intermediate
Period to take the place of magical
tomb wall scenes of food production and
offerings. Miniature wooden models of
various phases of food production replaced
the sculpted or painted wall scenes that
had hitherto guaranteed the nourishment
of the deceased. These dioramas were
commonplace in tombs. In one, a plank
with cursory wooden stick figures, two
women are shown bending over a low table
to roll out dough. A lidded storage jar for
flour separates them from a figure who
squats on the ground before an imaginary
fire, baking a stack of breads. A hive of

activity is indicated in another model, in which the diorama idea is further developed into a walled structure. A man enters through an open doorway with a vase on his head. Another bends to load a sack on his back, while yet another man is filling a sack. An overseer sits on a 'mezzanine' in the squatting position of a scribe, and records these activities on a large tablet on his knees, which may represent an open papyrus. In yet another diorama a bakery and a brewery are combined into a single model. Men approach from the right bearing the raw materials, while a man is bent over a large round vessel lid which he is using as a work table. Two more vessels flank him. In the background a woman squats on the ground before an imaginary fire and pile stack of bread. Behind her two other women are rolling out dough. In the foreground to the left of the scene a man is

standing up to grind something with a long pestle in a large open vat.

It is not clear whether terracotta models of houses with an open courtyard, known as 'soul houses', served the same purpose as the wooden dioramas. However, the fact that the courtyards of these houses are often filled with hand-modelled foodstuffs and animal parts may mean that they did indeed serve the same magical needs for the dead.

STATUETTE OF A NAKED LADY

Wood
Dimensions: 15,4 x 2,8 x 3,1 cm
Middle Kingdom, early Dynasty XII
(1976-1872 BC)
Provenance: Tomb of Shemes, Schiaparelli
excavations, Asyut, 1908
Inv. no. S. 8874

Women were not normally accorded their
own tombs. Mostly, they shared the tomb
of their spouse. Images of females in this
period were normally placed in men's tombs
as spouses, companions and servants.
The Egyptians did not as a rule represent
men and women as naked, but when they
did, scholars have wondered whether such
nude figures of women acted magically
as some sort of sexual companion for the
deceased. Indeed, some extant images of
females with legs abbreviated at the knee
lend credence to this theory, if one accepts
that they were modelled in his way so that
they could not escape the advances of the
deceased. Often such figures have other
overt sexual symbols, such as tattoos and
a girdle of cowry shells, very suggestive in
themselves. In the present image, however,
the woman has no such attributes and
has both legs. Her arms, which were
applied separately, no longer survive. The
unidentified lady wears her hair plaited
and bound around her head. What her
face lacks in definition, with the absence of
cosmetic rims and stripes, the sculptor has
made up for in the fine modelling of her
body. Although we cannot ascertain her age,
she has the idealised proportions of youth.
According to Egyptian convention, men
were modelled with the left leg advanced,
whereas women were usually represented
standing with their legs together. A tenon is
visible under the soles of the feet, showing
that this figure was once set on a base. In
some other cases at Asyut figures had been
wrapped in cloth, which may have been the
case here.

PALACE FAÇADE SARCOPHAGUS OF IBU

Limestone
Dimensions: 106 x 98,5 x 264,5 cm
Middle Kingdom, Dynasty XII (between
1976-1793 BC)
Provenance: Tomb of Ibu, Schiaparelli
excavations, Qaw el-Kebir, 1905-06
Inv. no. S. 4264

This limestone sarcophagus came to light
during Schiaparelli's excavations at Qaw
el-Kebir. The site housed the large and
impressive tomb complexes of Ibu, Wahka I,
Wahka II (brother of Ibu) and Sobek-Hotep,
officials of the Twelfth Dynasty. These tombs
were modelled on the pyramid complexes
composed of valley temple, causeway and
funerary temple with columned halls and
side chapels. This sarcophagus belonged to
the governor Ibu, called 'the thirsty one'. The
large rectangular monolithic coffin is carved
in relief on its sides with a series of false
doors. The fact that these are close together

recalls the traditional vertically stepped 'palace
façade' decoration. Some of the doors are
flanked by *ankh*, *djed* and *was*-symbols. The
largest, most elaborate, false door appears on
the long face, where the head of the deceased
was positioned lying on his left side. Here,
above an architrave, are the *wedjat*-eyes we
have previously encountered painted on the
exteriors of wooden coffins. A horizontal and
vertical inscription appears on every face of
the exterior, invoking the gods Osiris (east)
and Anubis (west) along with other minor
deities. The north and south short sides are
dedicated to the mourning sister goddesses
Nephtys and Isis respectively. The broken
monolithic lid is inscribed with various
prayer formulae derived from the 'Pyramid
Texts'. The two external inscriptions written
horizontally refer to the goddess Nut and
the owner of the coffin, whereas the text
facing east also mentions the sun god. Note
that the central formula is written with the
hieroglyphs running vertically. Fragmentary
life-size limestone heads of Ibu were also
recovered from the tomb.

TWO MIDDLE KINGDOM MALES

The man Ka (C. 3064)
Dimensions: 68 x 20 x 41 cm
Provenance unknown, later from the
Drovetti Collection, 1824

An anonymous male bust (S. 12010)
Dimensions: 20,8 x 16,2 x 10,2 cm

Provenance, Schiaparelli excavations,
Gebelein, 1910

Diorite
Middle Kingdom, late Dynasty XII
(1872-1793 BC)
Inv. nos. C. 3064, S. 12010

The royal house eventually fully re-established its sovereignty over the whole of Egypt and re-asserted its authority over the local families ruling from the provincial centres during the reign of King Sesostris III (1872-1853 BC) of the Twelfth Dynasty. It must have been a weary process, reflected in the king's image with deep-set eyes and heavy eyelids and strong downward pull at the corners of the mouth. As was the custom, the face of the king was imitated on statues of his courtiers and high officials, as exemplified by this seated figure of the treasurer Ka and another unidentified bust. In both cases, the eyes are deep set with half-closed lids. Although worn, the naso-labial furrows are evident. Both men wear a shoulder-length trapezoidal wig (a stylistic innovation for male figures of the Middle Kingdom) with large ears set high and flat against the wig, which has pushed them forwards. Both also wear a high-girt kilt, knotted at the midriff, which was also popular in this period. It is about this time that sculptures of private individuals, which hitherto only occurred in tombs, began to be dedicated in temples. The use of the hard stone diorite for both of these figures is significant, since it was not widely used during the previous long period of unrest and tension.

A FUNERARY STELE IN DIFFICULT TIMES

Painted limestone
Dimensions: 43 x 31 x 5,5 cm
Second Intermediate Period
(1646-1550 BC)
Provenance unknown, possibly the region of
Gebelein, acquired by Schiaparelli in Egypt,
1900-1901
Inv. no. S. 1281

It was not long before history repeated itself, so that the brief Middle Kingdom was followed by another decline in the king's power. The craft workshops shrank in size and standards and technical skill declined, though the number of private, small-format temple dedications increased. This funerary stele is a private commission of the period, roughly hewn and painted, not carved in relief, despite an incised contour of the chief figure. The images of the deceased and his wife, on a smaller scale, are painted on the left ('divine') side of the stele, both with unevenly shaped bodies. They are standing, in contrast to earlier stelae where the deceased couple is usually seated in front of a low table with four vases. The table appears to float above the baseline. A small female figure, perhaps the surviving daughter, is shown above offering incense, surrounded by various offerings. The rest of the free space above and between the figures is filled with a variety of food offerings. A brief prayer is inscribed below the patterned border. The directness of the imagery and the spiritual message is unmistakable; nourishment is offered to the deceased couple for the Afterlife. Eventually the royal workshops were revived and craftsmen were trained to the previous high standards.

A MAN AND A WOMAN OF THE EARLY NEW KINGDOM

Lady Suembenu (C. 3090)
Dimensions: 29,5 x 9 x 18 cm

A man (C. 3092)
Dimensions: 27 x 9 x 14,5 cm

Painted limestone
Early New Kingdom, Dynasty XVIII (about 1504-1425 BC)
Provenance: both probably from Deir el-Medina
Inv. nos. C. 3092, C. 3090

In the New Kingdom statues and statuettes of private individuals, both men and women, make their appearance as temple and chapel dedications and not just as figures interred in the tomb. These statuettes are modest, due to their choice of a soft limestone, which is more easily carved than hard stones like basalt. Characteristically for the period, the woman wears a long voluminous plaited wig, a colourful broad collar and a modest white tunic. Women were normally shown with pale skin, whereas men were depicted with a dark red skin tone. True to convention, this figure of the lady named Suembenu has a pale yellow complexion. Her chair, with its high back, provides a surface for a prayer and her name.

The red-skinned male figure has a short wig plaited in horizontal rows. A white cloat is draped asymmetrically over his left shoulder. Unlike the lady, whose hands both rest on her lap, he is holding in one hand a lotus flower against his chest. The stem of the lotus follows the contour of the cloak. However, we are meant to interpret this as the act of inhaling the intoxicating, even hallucinatory, pollen of the lotus, as also seen on stelae.

NEW KINGDOM STELAE

Djehutinefer and his wife Benbu (C. 1638)
Dimensions: 47,5 x 31,5 x 5 cm
Provenance: Dra Abu el-Naga, Thebes, later
Drovetti Collection, 1824

Mekhimontu and Nubemueskhet (S. 9492)
Dimensions: 28,5 x 20 x 4 cm
Provenance: Schiaparelli excavations, Thebes,
Deir el-Medina, 1909

Painted limestone
New Kingdom, early Dynasty XVIII
(1504-1479 BC)
Inv. nos. C. 1638, S. 9492

Whereas funerary monuments were normally
found underground in the tomb in the
Old Kingdom, these often appear above
ground in the New Kingdom. The round-
topped stelae (sing. stele), tended to follow
a visual formula. In these examples from the
early Eighteenth Dynasty two *wedjat*-eyes
symbolising the restored eye of the falcon
god Horus appear at the top, along with the
round *shen*-symbol (all that the sun encircles)
and the cup (for the verb 'to unite'). The
deceased couples sit on the left or 'divine'
side of the stele before an offering table. If
they have a surviving son or daughter, he or
she is usually depicted standing and facing
the couple on the right or 'living' side of the
stele, conducting the funeral rites.

On one stele Djehutinefer (whose nickname
is Seshu) and his wife Benbu are depicted in
low raised relief, seated on chairs with lion-
paw feet, with their young daughter, perhaps
also deceased, standing beside her parents'
chairs. An offering table is piled high with
food (a duck can be seen above the loaves of
bread). The couple is elegantly dressed, he
in an intricately plaited trapezoid wig, and a
fine white see-through tunic under a heavier
white kilt. Djehutinefer holds a sceptre of
office. Benbu is also dressed in a white tunic
with shoulder straps, and affectionately
embraces her husband. She is wearing a lotus
blossom (symbol of rebirth) circlet to hold
her long wig in place. Her young daughter
Neferty (with the side lock of a child) raises
the lotus blossom to her mother's nose. The
offerings and their numerical quantities are
carved on a raised block over the offering
table. The two main texts make up a prayer
to Harakhte and Osiris that the ba-souls of
the dead might enter heaven and the bodies
of the deceased might enter the Afterlife.

The stele of Mekhimontu and his wife
Nubemueskhet is very closely related to that
of Djehutinefer, with the difference that the
man is not holding a sceptre and so is able
to be represented smelling the intoxicating
lotus. The surviving brother standing at the
right, whose name is Smen, conducts the
libation ceremony.

AMENEMOPE OFFERS A STELE

Painted limestone
Dimensions: 55 x 20 x 26 cm
New Kingdom, Dynasty XVIII, probably
reign of Hatshepsut (1479-1458 BC)
Provenance: Theban area, later Drovetti
Collection, 1824
Inv. no. C. 3038

An innovation of the New Kingdom is the combination of sculpture and stele. This type is referred to by Egyptologists as a stelophoros (literally: stele-bearing) statue. Here the worker Amenemope, from the artisans' village at Deir el-Medina, kneels to offer a stele inscribed with a solar hymn to his god. Solar hymns were a genre normally addressed to the sun in one of its daily phases, which were then linked to life itself. In this way sunrise was connected with birth, day with the triumph of good over evil, and sunset with death and the promise of rebirth. Here Amenemope kneels with his hands raised, palms outwards, in a gesture of praise and prayer that is familiar from two-dimensional scenes before gods. It is a generic gesture, but in the case of sun worship is probably especially significant. The Egyptians were aware of the behaviour of baboons, which stood on their hind legs facing the sunrise with their front legs raised, palm outwards, while they made a lot of noise as if to greet the sun. We can read the statue as Amenemope greeting the sun and praising it by raising his hands. The stele or support for the hymn technically blocks his hands and makes it look to the modern eye as if Amenemope is simply holding a stele. He has a shoulder-length striated, two-layered wig, crimped at the ends. This is a new stylistic feature of the New Kingdom. He is wearing a large broad collar and a long simple kilt, painted white. As was the convention, his skin is painted dark red. Amenemope's face has long, almost straight eyebrows in raised relief and rims around the eyes that end in extremely long cosmetic stripes. He has a beaked nose, which resembles that of Queen Hatshepsut, perhaps the reigning sovereign. It is possible that the statue once stood in a chapel, perhaps even a household one, in Amenemope's home at Deir el-Medina.

KING THUTMOSE III

Diorite
Dimensions: 192 x 64 x 133 cm
New Kingdom, Dynasty XVIII, reign of
Thutmose III (1479-1425 BC)
Provenance: Thebes, later Drovetti
Collection, 1824
Inv. no. C. 1376

What distinguishes a king from an ordinary
man is primarily the presence of a *uraeus*
cobra at his brow. This important statue of
Thuthmose III is immediately identifiable
as royal by the cobra worn over the pleated
nemes-headdress. In addition, the king may
wear, as here, the royal tail (it is not known
whether it is that of a bull or a lion) between
his legs. On the plinth of the statue, carved
under the feet, are the bows representing the

nine foreign tribes and enemies of Egypt,
which the king tramples underfoot. The
great size of the statue and the hardness of
the stone testify to the importance of the
personage: royal and/or divine. Otherwise,
the king sits with his hands open and flat on
his lap, just like private individuals, and is
not holding any sceptre of power or *ankh*
symbol.

The sovereign is shown wearing the tripartite
shendyt-kilt, which as we have seen, private
individuals started to wear in the Middle
Kingdom. Here, however, it is decorated
with a zigzag decorated belt (a new stylistic
feature) and a central cartouche naming
him as 'King of Upper and Lower Egypt
Menkheperre, the perfect god, given life'.
The king's face is gentle and elegant with
its raised relief eyebrows and cosmetic

stripes. His benign smile contrasts starkly with the impassiveness of the face and the strong modelling of the muscular torso. The inscription on the throne, however, reminds us that he is the 'King of the Two Lands, beloved of the god Amun-Re, a king given life for eternity'. As a military expansionist, Thutmose III campaigned in Palestine, Syria, Mesopotamia and south into much of Nubia. The sides of his throne reinforce the concept of sovereignty over the two Egyptian lands by means of the lung and windpipe for the hieroglyphic phrase *sema tawy*, 'uniting the Two Lands'. A graffito on the front of the base declares 'Decouvert par J.P. Rifaud sculpteur au service de M. Drovetti a Thebes 1818'. This form of labelling is found on a number of the sculptures that Drovetti collected, possibly because he feared their theft by the agents of competing diplomatic consuls, all vying to sell their finds to the emerging European national museums.

ELLESIYA TEMPLE

Sandstone
Dimensions: façade 8,50 x 4,60 m; vestibule 5,5 x 3,5 m; cella 2 x 3 m
New Kingdom, Dynasty XVIII, reign of Thutmose III (1479-1425 BC)
Provenance: Ellesiya, Nubia. Donated by the Arab Republic of Egypt, 1966
Inv. no. S. 18016

This small temple was hewn into the desert sandstone, some two hundred kilometres south of Aswan, in Nubia. It was dedicated to the local gods Horus of Maiam and Satet of Aswan. Modelled in high relief, they flank King Thutmose III (1479-1425 BC) in the deep cult niche.

Thutmose III, an expansionist king, commissioned this chapel in the 51st and 52nd years of his reign, and provided priests for its operation and the maintenance of the cult. The purpose of the chapel was to pacify the Nubians by venerating their local deities, and at the same time merge them with Egyptian ones. The raised relief scenes inside the chapel show the king always facing in the direction of the sanctuary and making offerings to the gods, who face outwards. The gods reciprocate by granting life, kingship, and so forth.

During the heresy of the later Amarna

Period, when the traditional pantheon of gods was largerly abolished, officials of King Akhenaten defaced the figures of Amun (the chief god of the Theban capital city). Amun's images were re-carved later, during the reign of King Ramesses II (in the Nineteenth Dynasty), under the viceroy Setau. From the 6th century AD onwards the temple was used as a place of worship by Christians, as is evident from the pentagrams and crosses carved into the earlier scenes (which were probably covered over with plaster). The temple was presented to Italy in 1966, as a token of gratitude by the Arab Republic of Egypt for the support given during the Nubian salvage campaign, when monuments were threatened by the creation of Lake Nasser after the construction of the Aswan High Dam.

KING AMENHOTEP II

Red granite
Dimensions: 152 x 57 x 79 cm
New Kingdom, Dynasty XVIII, reign of
Amenhotep II (1428-1397 BC)
Provenance: Thebes (?), later Drovetti
Collection, 1824
Inv. no. C. 1375

King Amenhotep II reigned for possibly
thirty-five years, having started as coregent
with his father. He undertook several foreign
military campaigns, though probably only

consolidating previous gains. Amenhotep II
was known as a great sportsman and boasted
his feats as a huntsman, charioteer and
archer on a number of monuments. Indeed,
the king's powerful musculature is evident in
this sculpture. Normally the king stands or
sits, but rarely kneels. Amenhotep is offering
two wine jars on his knees in a gesture of
extreme humility to an unseen deity. Temple
wall decorations often include royal offerings
of cool refreshing water, wine or milk, in
vessels that were distinctive to the beverage.
So this statue relates an actual temple rite of
offering.

The king wears the *nemes*-headdress, a false
beard (supported by a chin strap) and the
tripartite *shendyt*-kilt (a kilt that allowed free
movement and is often worn in scenes of
warfare). The arch of the king's eyebrows and
the shape of the cosmetic stripes are similar
to the gentle features of his father King
Thutmose III.

Amenhotep II built a garden, a palace, several
shrines, one made of white alabaster, and a
large court in front of the eighth pylon at the
Karnak temple complex. He also built a bark
shrine at the Luxor Temple. His mummy was
found in a sarcophagus in his own tomb in
the Valley of the Kings (KV 35).

THE FUNERARY EQUIPMENT OF MERIT

Mask (S. 8473)
Linen cartonnage, gilded, with eyes inlaid
in obsidian, alabaster and blue glass; broad
collar inlaid with carnelian and glass
Dimensions: 36 x 34 x 52 cm

Mummy (S. 8471/01)
Human remains
Dimensions: 20 x 147 x 34 cm

Sarcophagus (S. 8470)
Wood
Dimensions: 58 x 199 x 80 cm

New Kingdom, Dynasty XVIII, reigns
of Amenhotep II, Thutmose IV and
Amenhotep III (1428-1351 BC)
Provenance: Schiaparelli excavations,

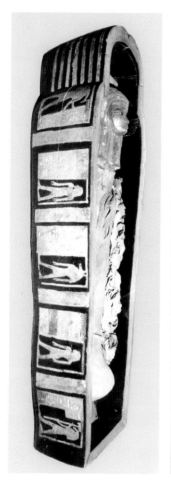

Deir el-Medina, 1906
Inv. nos. S. 8473, S. 8471/01, S. 8470

Generic facial features of the deceased were usually depicted not only on the lids of anthropoid coffins, but also on funerary masks, placed over the mummy's face. The preparation of the complete funerary equipment was a long process. This bust-length mask was actually intended for Kha, but his wife Merit predeceased him and so he used it for her, as he did with the coffin itself, which was ultimately too large for her. The mask is made of cartonnage composed of linen and plaster that was gilded and inlaid with glass details (blue stripes for the hair, darker blue for the eyebrows and cosmetic stripes and *wesekh*-collar). The fact that Kha himself was never provided with a mask suggests that it was an expensive undertaking. His anthropoid coffin, made to his dimensions, was hastily adapted for Merit and padded out with rolled textiles inserted around the mummy. The sides of the coffin are covered in black pitch and decorated with gilt figures representing the funerary gods along with protective texts on gilt panels. The lid is gilded in its entirety. The mummy, mask and inner coffin were placed in a larger shrine-shaped sarcophagus covered in black bitumen.

Ernesto Schiaparelli discovered the remarkably well-furnished tomb in 1906, but some of the traditional funerary objects were not included. For instance, there were no canopic jars for Merit or for Kha. Their internal organs are still in the bodies. Merit had no *shawabti*-figures. In fact only two *shawabti*-figures inscribed for Kha, as opposed to the hundreds normally found in well-equipped private tombs of a later period, were included. It is not clear what implications should be drawn from these omissions. On the other hand, radiography has shown that Merit's body is adorned with numerous gold jewels, that cannot be extracted due to the fact that their removal would damage the mummy bindings.

KHA'S BOOK OF THE DEAD

Papyrus
Dimensions: 35 x 1380 cm
New Kingdom, Dynasty XVIII, reigns
of Amenhotep II, Thutmose IV and
Amenhotep III (1428-1351 BC)
Provenance: Tomb of Kha, Schiaparelli
excavations, Deir el-Medina, 1906
Inv. no. S. 8438

The so-called *Book of the Dead* was a text
written on a long papyrus subsequently
used by the deceased as a magical guide
through the Netherworld. It was usually
written either in hieroglyphs, as in this
case, (or in hieratic script), in vertical
columns or horizontal lines, sometimes
with illustrations. The formulae are
derived from more ancient funerary
texts such as the Pyramid and Coffin
Texts, Judgement in the Afterlife and
Sun Hymns. The choice from more than
a hundred possible chapters of the *Book
of the Dead* was often an individual one.
For the sequence of the chapters, scholars
tend to rely on a long text written in
the Ptolemaic Period, now in the Museo

Egizio, although this was never formalized
in antiquity.

This *Book of the Dead* was found folded on
Kha's middle coffin. It comprises over 30
chapters written in 200 columns of text in
which Kha is named about a hundred times.
The book begins with a scene of the worship
of Osiris. Kha and his wife Merit wear white
garments, have white wax perfume cones on
their heads, and stand with hands raised in
an attitude of praise before the shrine of the
god Osiris, King of the Netherworld. Osiris
is depicted as a royal mummy holding a flail
(possibly a ruler's fly whisk), a *was*-sceptre,
symbolising power, and a crook for his
pastoral role. A table piled high with food
offerings stands before the shrine. The
chapters deal with the transformation of the
souls and bodies of the deceased.

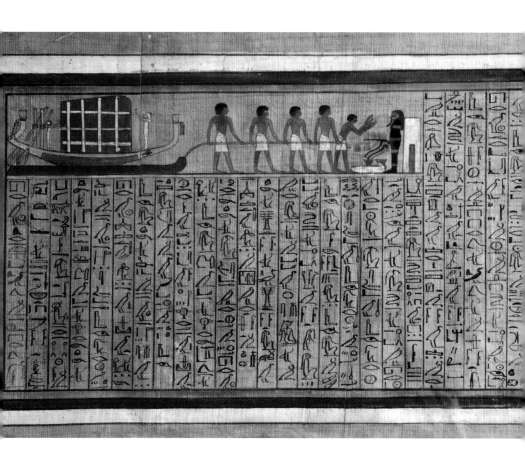

CHAIR AND STATUETTE OF KHA

Statuette (S. 8333)
Dimensions: 48 x 12 x 27,5 cm

Chair (S. 8335)
Dimensions: 91 x 44,5 x 55,5 cm

Painted wood
New Kingdom, Dynasty XVIII, reigns
of Amenhotep II, Thutmose IV and
Amenhotep III (1428-1351 BC)
Provenance: Tomb of Kha, Schiaparelli
excavations, Deir el-Medina, 1906
Inv. nos. S. 8333, S. 8335

In this period one would normally expect
to find canopic jars for the internal organs
and *shawabti*-figures. Remarkably, Kha
and his wife had no canopic jars. As for the
shawabti-figures, there were only two in the
tomb and these were for Kha.
A single statuette of Kha, along with the
two smaller *shawabti*-figures, a miniature
hoe and a model sarcophagus were placed
on the high-backed chair alongside Merit's
sarcophagus of. According to Schiaparelli,
the fact that the wooden statuette, the only
existing sculpture of Kha, was placed on the
chair was meant to signify ownership of the
throne. The excavator also remarked that
the chair was probably a reproduction for
the tomb of an actual chair with more costly
black-and-white intarsia inlays of ebony and
ivory. Lotus blossoms and buds, clusters of
grapes and running spirals are painted on the
upper back of the chair. The black lion's feet
were meant to imitate finer examples made
of hammered bronze sheet. The seat is woven
from fibre cords.

The statuette depicts Kha with his hands
lowered and with his palms resting on the
apron of his kilt in a sign of humility.
He wears a shoulder-length wig of two
layers, striated at the top and plaited below.
A garland of small real flowers adorns the
chest of the figure and another has fallen
onto the base. The funerary prayer text in
yellow pigment appears in a column on the
front of the kilt and on the rectangular base.

A WOODEN COFFER

Painted wood
Dimensions: 35 x 48 x 34 cm
New Kingdom, Dynasty XVIII, reigns
of Amenhotep II, Thutmose IV and
Amenhotep III (1428-1351 BC)
Provenance: Tomb of Kha, Schiaparelli
excavations, Deir el-Medina, 1906
Inv. no. S. 8213

There was a total of sixteen wooden coffers
in Kha's tomb, some of them small, for eye
makeup (kohl), some larger for bedding
and the largest of all for Merit's wig. This
wooden coffer with its double-pitched
sliding lid is covered with a multitude of
colourful decorative schemes. A scene on one
of the long sides illustrates Kha and Merit
seated on high-backed chairs, like the one
found in the tomb, before an offering table
piled high with food. Their son, wearing a
kilt and a long thin tunic, stands on the left
and offers a bunch of lotus flowers to the
couple, who are elevated on a green pedestal
decorated with vertical stripes. All the figures
wear white perfume cones on their heads.
The scene is framed by vertical bands of
trompe l'oeil grained wood and by a frieze of
inverted pointed white leaves along the top
edge. Nine columns of text above the figures
identify the offerings and the persons.

The opposite long side is decorated with a
chequerboard pattern and a central rectangle
with *trompe l'oeil* grained wood. The short
sides are decorated with a diamond pattern
with five-pointed stars in each cell. The
pitched roof, which slides along a dovetailed
central rail, is decorated on one side with
a frieze of rosettes and zigzags in different
colours, and on the other side with a line of
text and bands of pointed leaves, lotus buds
and blossoms. The coffer contained two
linen tunics and two large pieces of cloth.
The coffer was closed with a cord wound in
a 'figure of eight' between the mushroom-
shaped knob on the pediment of the lid and
another similar one on the short side.

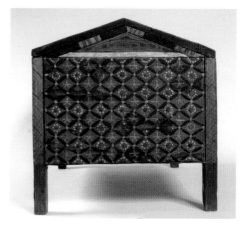

TOILET BOX

Wood (sycamore) with alabaster, glass and
faience vessels
Dimensions: S. 8479: 22 x 29,5 x 49 cm;
S. 8480: 9,6 x 7,6 cm; S. 8481: 13 x 6,9 cm;
S. 8483: 5,5 x 6,7 cm; S. 8484: 7,6 x 7 cm;
S. 8486: 9,8 x 9 cm; S. 8487: 13 x 6,1 cm;
S. 8489: 9,2 x 3,7 cm; S. 8490: 8,3 x 5,4 cm
New Kingdom, Dynasty XVIII, reigns
of Amenhotep II, Thutmose IV and
Amenhotep III (1428-1351 BC)
Provenance: Tomb of Kha, Schiaparelli
excavations, Deir el-Medina, 1906
Inv. nos. S. 8479, S. 8480, S. 8481, S. 8483,
S. 8484, S. 8486, S. 8487, S. 8489, S. 8490

Among Merit's equipment in the tomb was
her beauty case. The wooden box blazes
in a riot of patterns: the front and lid with
a green, white and yellow chequerboard
pattern, the sides with a black-and-white
imitation of ivory and ebony intarsia and a
frieze of lotus buds and blossoms. The box
was fitted with five compartments inside to
hold the ointment and vessels for kohl. Both
were regarded as a necessary part of hygiene,
and here they were kept in a variety of
receptacles composed of different materials.
Some of the vessels are alabaster, two are
glass (a rare and precious material for the
period), one is faience and one is made of
an animal tusk. The Egyptians wore black
kohl under the eyes (also depicted as a long

cosmetic stripe on sculptures) in order to
protect themselves from flies and sunlight.
One glass kohl vessel here is shaped like a
palm tree, which as a hieroglyph signifies 'to
be young'.

At this early date glass vessels were not yet
blown, but were made by winding coils of
hot glass over a core of organic material and
then rolling it over a flat surface. Glass of
different colours was 'trailed' over the surface
and then dragged with a metal tool into
zigzag designs. The earliest attested glass in
Egypt dates from the reign of Thutmose III
(1479-1425 BC). The inscription on the
front of this box, possibly added just before
burial, makes it clear that the beauty case is a
funerary offering for Merit's spirit.

MERIT'S WIG AND WIG BOX

Wig (S. 8499)
Human hair
Length: 54 cm

Wig Box (S. 8493)
Wood
Dimensions: 111 x 49,3 x 49 cm

New Kingdom, Dynasty XVIII, reigns
of Amenhotep II, Thutmose IV and
Amenhotep III (1428-1351 BC)
Provenance: Deir el-Medina, from the tomb
of Kha, Schiaparelli excavations, 1906
Inv. nos. S. 8499, S. 8493

All women of rank wore elaborate wigs.
Merit's wig is made of long human hair
(about 54 cm) arranged with a central
parting and crimped tresses that are plaited
at the ends. Two thick and long plaits appear
at the back and two thin plaits framed the
face. An elaborate inner system of knots
and weaves holds the different parts of the
wig together. This 'enveloping hair style', in
which the ears were covered, was popular
during the second half of the Eighteenth
Dynasty. Merit is depicted wearing this type
of wig in the first scene of the *Book of the
Dead* papyrus.

The wooden box which once held Merit's
wig is shaped like a shrine. The sloping lid
shuts against a palmetto moulding. The
box was locked by a cord wound in a 'figure
of eight' between the mushroom-shaped
knob on the lid and another similar one
on the front panel, and then sealed with a
mud stamp. The cavetto moulding, with its
alternating coloured bars, is finished only on
one side. A brief funerary offering formula is
inscribed on the lid: 'A funerary offering to
Osiris, the great God, Lord of Eternity, that
he may make an offering of an ox, birds and
everything to the spirit of Merit'. The sides
of the box are composed of different kinds
of wood (the front and right face seem to be
of a finer quality). The decoration is sketchy,
with a geometrical net motif on the back
(and on one side) with an unfinished scene
of a man offering to a seated couple, and a
scene of lamentation. A funerary offering
formula for the spirit of Merit appears on
the front. Two parallel wooden crossbeams
on the inside, both covered by a linen cloth,
held Merit's wig. A few plaits of hair and
strands became detached and were found on
the floor of the wig box.

BOARD GAME

Wood
Dimensions: 9 x 13,5 x 43 cm
New Kingdom, Dynasty XVIII, reigns of
Amenhotep II, Thutmose IV and
Amenhotep III (1428-1351 BC)
Provenance: Tomb of Kha, Schiaparelli
excavations, Deir el-Medina, 1906
Inv. no. S. 8451

The board game *senet* was played throughout
Egyptian history, but few complete sets survive.
This game from Kha's tomb has the form of
a hollow wooden box with a drawer for the
gaming pieces. The top of the box is carved into a
chequerboard pattern of twelve cells and a further
central extension of eight cells. Two groups
of gaming pieces shaped like spools (five in
number) and cones (seven) were included. Like
many modern board games, *senet* was played by
two people using a set of dice, in this case made
of animal knucklebones. Placed in the tomb, the
game of *senet* took on a serious meaning, because
according to Chapter 17 of the *Book of the Dead*
the winner of the game would emerge with a
living *ba*-soul.

The drawer of this set is equipped with a sliding
bolt that prevented it from opening inadvertently
when the game was being carried around.

AN ANCIENT CAMP STOOL

Wood with ebony and ivory inlay,
leather seat
Dimensions: 54 x 87 x 37 cm
New Kingdom, Dynasty XVIII, reigns
of Amenhotep II, Thutmose IV and
Amenhotep III (1428-1351 BC)
Provenance: Deir el-Medina, from the tomb
of Kha, Schiaparelli excavations, 1906
Inv. no. S. 8509

As in every high-status household, outdoor
seating was necessary. Considering Kha's
station in life, it is not surprising that he
had an elegant folding stool, which he used
on country excursions. This wooden stool
had a leather seat that was stretched between
two crossbars. The four legs of the stool
terminate in sculpted duck heads, whose
details are inlaid with ebony and ivory. On
less luxurious models, such detailing would
normally have been painted. The legs are
connected by two rounded splints, clenched
in the ducks' beaks, to make the stool
steadier. The four legs cross so that the chair
can be folded up and put away.

'camp stools', are known from the Middle
Kingdom. Later their use became widespread
in high society and in court circles.

A short hieroglyphic inscription in black ink
on one of the two base splints identifies Kha,
'Overseer of Works', as the owner of this
prestigious folding stool. Such seats, used as

TWO-HANDLED VASE

Ceramic, painted and covered with linen
that is also painted
Dimensions: 39 x 23 cm
New Kingdom, Dynasty XVIII, reigns
of Amenhotep II, Thutmose IV and
Amenhotep III (1428-1351 BC)
Provenance: Tomb of Kha, Schiaparelli
excavations, Deir el-Medina, 1906
Inv. no. S. 8619

There were distinctive shapes for both
pottery and stone vessels in every period,
probably connected with their contents.
This vase is essentially globular with a long-
handled neck ending in a splayed rim. It is
not immediately evident, but the long neck
is actually completely covered by a fabric
that is the same colour as the buff pottery. It
is decorated with green papyrus plants and
typical religious-funerary symbols: a black-
and-white painted *wedjat*-eye and a black
neb-symbol surmounted by three yellow-
and-white *nefer*-symbols. The decoration
can be read as 'all good and healthy things'.
The shoulder with chevrons in the same
colour scheme creates a feather-like motif.
A single lotus is painted on each handle
with stylized green leaves. The long neck
would have slowed evaporation, but to
ensure that the contents were preserved,
the vessel was closed with narrow strips of
fabric plaited together in a geometric pattern
and tied tightly under the rim. It is possible
that the vessel once contained wine, highly
appreciated by those who could afford the
good life.

FAIENCE BOWLS

Bowl with lotus flowers (C. 3369)
Dimensions: 13 x 4,4 cm

Bowl with Hathor heads (C. 3368)
Dimensions: 16,5 x 5 cm

Faience, decorated with manganese black
New Kingdom (about 1350 BC)
Provenance unknown, later Drovetti
Collection, 1824
Inv. nos. C. 3369, C. 3368

Beautiful blue faience, a siliceous material,
served as the perfect background for Nilotic
imagery. Thus faience bowls appeared in the
New Kingdom decorated with lotus buds
and blossoms and the ubiquitous bolti fish
in manganese black, the colour used for the
fertile soil of Egypt. The bolti, which is still
found in the Nile today, was venerated in
Egypt as a symbol of rebirth and autogenesis.
This was because it swallows its eggs until
they are hatched. The fish was therefore
associated with the transformation of the

dead, and was a potent symbol of fertility.
The lotus, which blossoms at dawn and
closes at dusk, figured as a regenerative
symbol, appropriate for tomb furnishings. It
has been suggested that this type of faience
bowl signified the primaeval watery abyss
from which the cosmos (Egypt) emerged.
The decoration inside is wholly appropriate
for the tomb.

THE GODDESS HATHOR

Basalt
Dimensions: 153 x 47 x 35 cm
New Kingdom, Dynasty XVIII, reign of
Amenhotep III (1388-1351 BC)
Provenance: originally Coptos, later
Donati Collection
Inv. no. C. 694

Hathor, the celestial cow whose headdress comprises horns and a sun disk, was a mother goddess. Indeed, she is sometimes shown with cow's ears. The name Hathor, literally 'House of Horus', implies that she was the wet nurse of the god Horus, incarnated as the ruling king of Egypt. In the Late Period Hathor was assimilated with Isis, mother of Horus, so that it becomes difficult to distinguish between them. Hathor was a joyful goddess, and as such was the mistress of dance, music and love. This figure was commissioned by King Amenhotep III to celebrate his jubilee (*sed*-festival) at Coptos. Although much of Egyptian sculpture may look similar to the casual observer, some features here are distinctive of the style of Amenhotep III. The arched shape of the ribbon-like eyebrows and the dip of the inner corners of the almond-shaped eyes are characteristic of sculptures of the king and especially of his wife Queen Tiye.
So too are the prominent lips under a well-defined philtrum. The enlarged earlobes, on which an indentation features to suggest piercing, are a characteristic feature which would become common on images of both sexes during this and the subsequent reign of the 'heretic' King Akhenaten. Unusually, the goddess holds a *was*-sceptre symbolizing power, normally held by male deities, in place of the more usual papyrus *wadj*-sceptre, reserved for goddesses. This sculpture was brought to Turin by Professor Vitaliano Donati, a botanist commissioned by King Charles Emanuel III of Savoy in 1753 to acquire objects in Egypt, seventy-one years before the purchase of the large Drovetti Collection.

THE GOD PTAH

Diorite
Dimensions: 207 x 62 x 76 cm
New Kingdom, Dynasty XVIII, reign of
Amenhotep III (1388-1351 BC)
Provenance: originally Thebes, later
Drovetti Collection, 1824
Inv. no. C. 86

As in all cultures, myths were devised to explain the universe and its creation. The Egyptians used their greatest technological advance, the potter's wheel, as a means of describing the creation of man. Although mythology and iconography are vague when it comes to Ptah, there is a corpus of coffin texts that describe him as the creator god and divine artist. Even his name might mean 'fashioner'. As a creation deity, Ptah was the patron of craftsmen and wore the close-fitting cap and straight beard of craftsmen and smiths. He is one of the few Egyptian gods who does not have a manifestation as an animal. His close-fitting sheath garment resembles mummy wrappings, and have not been explained sufficiently. The centre of Ptah's cult was the city of Memphis. His consort was Sakhmet and together they were the parents of Nefertum, the deity of scent. Ptah's association with Memphis played a role in his assimilation with the local god of the Netherworld, Sokar. From the Middle Kingdom onwards Ptah, Sokar and Osiris were united as a single god of the Netherworld. Later Ptah was called the father of the Apis bull, who conveyed the deceased to the Netherworld. Ptah's creative qualities resulted in his association with the legendary architect Imhotep, who is supposed to have designed the pyramid of Djoser.

Here, the god holds his two attributes: the *was*-sceptre of power, and the *djed*-column, derived from the backbone of the god Osiris and visually forming the word for 'to endure'. In addition, he holds an *ankh*, the symbol of life, in each fist. The inscription on the statue commisioned by King Amenhotep III names Ptah as 'elected by Re, the lord of justice and jubilees who resides in the Hall of Annals'. The inscription confirms the dating on the grounds of style, the statue having the arched eyebrows and inwardly slanted rimmed eyes, and long cosmetic stripes at the corners that are similar to the features of the figure of the goddess Hathor in this museum, also datable to the reign of King Amenhotep III.

THE GODDESS SAKHMET

Standing Sakhmet (C. 265)
Dimensions: 210 x 46 x 36 cm

Seated Sakhmet (C. 253)
Dimensions: 213 x 51 x 105 cm

Diorite
New Kingdom, Dynasty XVIII, reign of
Amenhotep III (1388-1351 BC)
Provenance: Thebes, Karnak / Temple of
Amenhotep III (possibly re-used at the
Temple of Mut)
Inv. nos. C. 253, C. 265

The lion-headed goddess Sakhmet of Memphis
was Ptah's wife. She was an avenging, fire-spitting
goddess who helped to vanquish foreign
enemies. Her connection with fire resulted in
her association with the *uraeus*-cobra worn on
the king's forehead. Another attribute of hers is
the solar disk.
As Thebes was the capital of Egypt during the
early New Kingdom, it was necessary for the
consort of the chief god Amun to be a woman
of great substance. Thus, the goddess Mut,
hitherto Amun's wife, was assimilated with the
powerful and popular Sakhmet.

To celebrate this new version of the goddess,
hundreds of her statues were set up at the
Temple of Karnak, mostly in the area dedicated
to Mut. Hundreds of others may have originally
stood at the funerary temple of Amenhotep III
located on the west bank of the Nile. Perhaps
365, the number of days in the Egyptian
calendar, were sculpted standing, and the same
number seated.
These numbers give us an idea of the
sculptural output of the ateliers of a single
king. Naturally, Sakhmet was not the only
deity that Amenhotep III had sculpted, so one
can imagine the size of the workshops and the
pace at which the sculptors worked. Indeed,
excavators have recently located many more
figures at Amenhotep's funerary temple (near
the so-called Colossi of Memnon). Some of the
figures from Amenhotep's funerary temple were
possibly dragged later to the east side of the river
at Karnak for a second use at the Mut temple.

Scholars are divided over the question of the
date of production for all these figures, though
the figures with rosettes carved in relief on
the breasts may be datable to the reign of
Amenhotep III. The Museo Egizio has twenty-
one in all, ten seated, and eleven standing
versions of the goddess without inscriptions.

THE TREASURER AND PROPHET ANEN

Diorite
Dimensions: 146 x 38,5 x 57 cm
New Kingdom, Dynasty XVIII, reign of
Amenhotep III (1388-1351 BC)
Provenance: originally Thebes, later
Drovetti Collection, 1824
Inv. no. C. 1377

King Amenhotep III elevated his brother-in-law Anen (the brother of Queen Tiye) to important positions, which included Treasurer of Lower Egypt and Second Prophet of the temple of the god Amun. Anen was not only well connected, but also knowledgeable in the field of astronomy, as confirmed by the five-pointed-star decoration of the panther skin he wears over his shoulder. According to the inscription, Anen was in fact an accomplished astronomer and seer. Although priests normally had a shaven head, Anen wears a stylish wig, typical of the period, which is crimped and plaited in two layers. The panther skin also alludes to his clerical role. The elaborate bag hanging from his belt probably refers to his office as treasurer. The royal seal within the bag relates to his secular role as 'Holder of the Royal Seal'.

The face is badly worn, yet the traces of the arched brows and the slanted eyes are typical of the reign of King Amenhotep III. In this period private statues could be set up in tombs or in temples and small chapels. The votive statues were meant to guarantee an eternal connection between the devotee and the deity, whereas the funerary type was intended to serve as a substitute body for the *ka* of the deceased. By placing his statue in the Amun temple at Karnak, Anen assured himself a lasting presence in the sight of the god. Anen's name was carved in several places on the statue in order to keep his memory alive.

QUEEN TIYE AS THE GODDESS TAWERET

Wood, traces of gilding and red bole, plaster on the modius, Egyptian blue in the chevron decoration of the crocodile tail, black pigment on the wig and eyes
Dimensions: 15 x 5,5 x 5,5 cm
New Kingdom, Dynasty XVIII, reign of Amenhotep III (1388-1351 BC)
Provenance unknown
Inv. no. C. 566

In addition to the official pantheon of gods, there were other, lesser deities. Taweret was a folk goddess, depicted as a hybrid pregnant hippopotamus standing upright on leonine legs. She is shown with post-natal breasts, human arms terminating in lion's paws, and the spine and tail of a crocodile. In this wooden figurine the hippopotamus's head is replaced by the beautiful head of a queen. She wears a long, intricately striated and stepped wig, bound by a wide circlet which

was originally gilded. A hole in the forehead marks the point where a *uraeus*-cobra, no doubt made of another material, was inserted separately. Surmounting the head is a modius that served as a base for a plumed headdress.

The face of the queen displays the unmistakable features of Queen Tiye, consort of Amenhotep III. Her eyes slant down towards the root of the nose, under naturally formed lids in a long shallow orbit. Cosmetic stripes of black paint extend as far as the ears, whose lobes are indented to indicate piercing, another characteristic of the period. She also has the fleshy, heart-shaped mouth typical for this reign.

Taweret was a goddess of marriage, a protector of women, especially in childbirth and in child-rearing, and as such she shared traits with the goddess Hathor. Queen Tiye was worshipped as a living goddess, and was variously associated with Taweret, Hathor and Maat.

KING AKHENATEN AND THE AMARNA STYLE

Limestone
Dimensions: 10 x 5 x 7 cm
New Kingdom, Dynasty XVIII, reign of
Akhenaten (1351-1334 BC)
Provenance unknown, probably Tel el-
Amarna, later Drovetti Collection, 1824,
purchased
Inv. no. C. 1398

Akhenaten, son of King Amenhotep III,
was the earliest apostate in history, who
dismantled the established pantheon of
deities and its powerful priesthood. The king
chose to worship only the Aten sun disk.
He moved his court away from Thebes, and
founded a new city named after his god
Akhetaten, 'Horizon of the Aten' (modern
Tel el-Amarna). The Amarna Period (named
after the site) introduced an innovative
naturalistic artistic style.

This miniature head of King Akhenaten
depicts the pharaoh with the so-called Blue
Crown or *khepresh*, which lent itself to the
artistic tendency to depict the skull as if it
had been stretched. Indeed, the dimensions of
the helmet-like war crown, normally shorter
and more upright, have been altered from
those of previous reigns to accommodate the
elongated skull of the king. Scholars have
often discussed whether the shape of the head
is due to a birth deformity or to binding in
infancy. The typical features of Akhenaten,
such as the long face with naturally formed
lidded eyes set into orbits under the ridge
of the brows, are evident. His nose is long
and thin, whereas his mouth is fleshy and
heart-shaped. The lobes of the ears have been
indented horizontally to show they were
pierced. This feature, noted from the reign of
King Amenhotep III, continued well into the
Ramesside Period, before it disappeared from
male figures altogether. The head has been
carved in such a way that it almost appears
unfinished, but the 'blurred' treatment of the
eyes in particular was one of many approaches
to facial modelling during the reign.

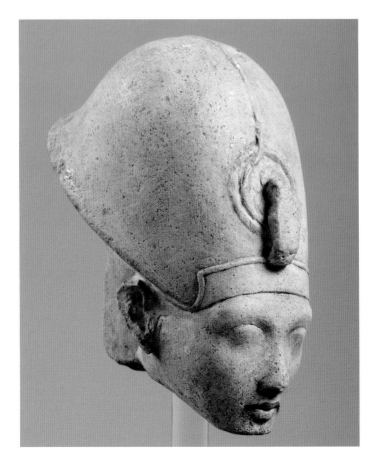

TALATAT RELIEFS FROM THE CITY OF TEL EL-AMARNA

Relief of a man and a cow (S. 18142)
Limestone, with modern pigment
Dimensions: 22 x 34 cm
Provenance: acquired 1970

Relief of musicians (S. 18060)
Limestone, sunk relief
Dimensions: 22 x 27 cm
Provenance: acquired 1969

New Kingdom, Dynasty XVIII, reign of
Akhenaten (1351-1334 BC)
Inv. nos. S. 18142, S. 18060

The city of Akhetaten (today known as Tel
el-Amarna) was built in great haste in Middle
Egypt at a site not hitherto occupied. The walled
city had a number of open-air chapels which
served the royal family, who worshipped the
sun directly and passed on its beneficence to the
citizens. The stone blocks for the temples were
quarried and cut in a new size that was roughly
the length of three open palms, known today
as *talatat* deriving from the Arabic word for the
number three. In the newly built city, artists
were encouraged to experiment, and as a result,
successive registers of stiff figures firmly rooted
to the baselines were abandoned.

In one *talatat* here, a man is depicted in sunk
relief facing rightwards, with rounded shoulders
in a kind of adjusted perspective so that the right
arm (close to the viewer's plane) crosses the body

in order to stroke a calf. A similar perspective
adjustment has been made with the crescent
horns of the cow, perhaps to indicate that its
head is tilted slightly to receive this gesture
of tenderness. Moments of affection towards
animals were not part of the usual repertoire of
Egyptian art. The space around the figures and
the lack of an inscription are characteristic of
such Amarna scenes.

In another *talatat*, a group of women with arms
raised, one with a tambourine, is making music.
The female contour takes on a new shape during
the Amarna Period. Just as the king was depicted
with a high waist, long back and thick thighs, so
too women of the reign were shown with high
midriffs and gently swelling bellies and hips. The
interplay of raised and sunk relief resulting from
the overlap of the figures at uneven intervals is
a characteristic of *talatat* decoration. The gap
between this cluster of women and the traces of
two figures of differing size behind them, makes
it apparent that the artisans felt it important
to provide these figures with empty space
within which to create the illusion of a forward
movement.

This stele started life as a block decorated in sunk relief set in a wall at Tel el-Amarna, but was reused some two hundred years later, when it was reshaped as a stele for a certain Pentauret. The original Amarna carving remains visible on the side of the stele. A papyrus thicket appears on the left thickness of the stele near a small image of the Aten sun disk, whose rays shine upon a doorway. Further along is a doorway opening onto a columned hall, shown in section. Two palm-shaped columns are draped with banners. The hall must have been a large one, spanning three storeys, as can be inferred from the three superimposed doorways further along to the left.

The block was cut into the form of a round-topped stele for Pentauret, who is shown standing on the right on another face, with his arms upraised in a gesture of adoration before the god Osiris, seated on the left or 'divine' side of the stele. Between the two figures is a remarkable lotus that functions as a table and is surmounted by the four canopic deities. The scene continues in the register below with three family worshippers also praising Osiris.

STELE OF PENTAURET

Limestone
Dimensions: 46 x 22 x 12 cm
New Kingdom, Dynasty XVIII, reign of
Akhenaten (1351-1334 BC), re-carved in
Dynasty XIX (1292-1186 BC)
Provenance unknown, probably Tel el-Amarna
Inv. no. C. 1563

TOMB CHAPEL AND STELE OF MAIA AND HIS WIFE

Chapel (S. 7919)
Plastered and painted mud brick
Dimensions: 185 x 145 x 225 cm
Provenance: Deir el-Medina, TT 338,
Schiaparelli excavations, 1905

Stele (C. 1579)
Limestone
Dimensions: 66,7 x 42 x 7,3 cm
Provenance: Deir el-Medina, TT 338, later
Drovetti Collection, 1824

New Kingdom, late Dynasty XVIII
(1350-1292 BC)
Inv. nos. S. 7919, C. 1579 (CGT 50009)

In the New Kingdom, the tomb was normally underground and closed following the burial. The family and priests were able to 'visit' the deceased in the above-ground funerary chapel nearby, where the rites took place. In the case of Maia and his wife Tamit, their funerary stele was found by Drovetti in their funerary chapel and brought to the Museum in 1824. The couple appears in white garments, praising Osiris and Hathor in the top register of the stele, and in the one below they are shown seated before an offering table, receiving food from their nine children, each of whom is named. A small tenth child appears under her parents' chair.

The offering chapel is comparable in size to that of Kha, who cleverly had his tomb dug some distance away from the chapel, thus foiling any possible attempt at tomb robbery. The chapel of Maia and Tamit, probable contemporaries of Kha, is decorated on three registers with the funerary procession, protected by amulets, as well as the transport of the funerary equipment, and the ritual voyage to Abydos. Maia's parents also make their appearance on the end wall of the chapel. Two of Maia's sons conduct the funerary rites of censing and libation.

It was Ernesto Schiaparelli who transferred the painted walls of the chapel to Turin in 1905.

GROUP SCULPTURE OF THE PHARAOH WITH THE GOD AMUN

Limestone
Dimensions: 209 x 90 x 112 cm
New Kingdom, Dynasty XVIII, probably
reign of Tutankhamun (1333-1323 BC)
Provenance: probably Thebes, later Drovetti
Collection, 1824
Inv. no. C. 768

Following the Amarna heresy, King
Tutankhamun restored the traditional
religion and its divine pantheon, and
declared his allegiance to Amun, the god of
the Theban capital. In this double sculpture
in white limestone, the king demonstrates
his subordination to the god in a number of
ways. The king's smaller dimensions and his
location to the left of the god, his lack of a
tall crown (other than the *nemes*-headcloth)
and the fact that he is standing, whereas the
god is sitting, all combine to underline the
concept of submission. The king shows
his love by embracing the god, but this
gesture is not reciprocated by Amun,
whose left hand is occupied, grasping
the *ankh*-symbol of life. Stylistically the
sculpture still owes a debt to the Amarna
Period. The figures' eyes are carved in
sunken orbits with hooded eyelids, unlike
the pre-Amarna faces, flatly carved on
a single plane. The king's waist is high,
his abdomen swells over a low-slung kilt
and his thighs are thick, according to the
Amarna ideal. On stylistic grounds, this
group of statues is attributed to King
Tutankhamun, although his name does
not appear on them. Instead, the sculpture
is inscribed with the name of the later
King Haremhab, and probably signifies a
usurpation of his predecessor's statue.

KING HAREMHAB AND QUEEN MUTNEDJEMET

Black granite
Dimensions: 139 x 86 x 92 cm
New Kingdom, Dynasty XVIII, reign of
Haremhab (1319-1292 BC)
Provenance: probably Thebes, later Drovetti
Collection, 1824
Inv. no. C. 1379

King Haremhab and his wife Mutnedjemet, whose name refers to Mut, wife of the god Amun, are represented in this group sculpture. Unfortunately, due to the loss of the king's head and the poor preservation of his wife's face, and the fact that there are no other sculptures reliably attributed to this king, it is not possible to establish his iconography and eventual debt to the Amarna style. The partially preserved figure of the king wears the *nemes*-headdress and carries the royal flail. The queen wears the double *uraeus* on her plaited wig, which is smooth where a vulture headdress would

have been applied in gold sheet. On the side of her seat, a sphinx is depicted adoring the cartouche enclosing her name. On the king's side of the seat four bound prisoners, two of them Asian and two Nubian, are represented, underlining Haremhab's supremacy over their lands.

A long, twenty-six-line inscription on the back slab, gives an account of Haremhab's military and civil career. Before he ascended to the throne he was not only a scribe but also Director of Works and King's Deputy during the reigns of Tutankhamun and Aye. The text repeatedly invokes the god Amun in order to establish Haremhab's credentials as a traditionalist, following the Amarna heresy of sun worship. The king planned to be buried in the north at Saqqara, where he built his tomb as a high-ranking official, but after his coronation, another far more elaborate tomb (KV 57) was commissioned for him in the Valley of the Kings in the western Theban necropolis.

Late New Kingdom (1300-1200 BC); faience *shawabti*: Late Period (7th – 4th century BC)
Provenance unknown, later Drovetti Collection, 1824
Inv. nos. C. 2600, C. 2806, C. 2666, C. 2509, C. 2444

In Egypt everyone, both the living and the dead, was expected to work the land following the Nile flood. In the Middle Kingdom, *shawabti*-figures were devised and inserted in tombs in order to 'answer the call to work'. These *shawabti*-figures are usually mummiform and hold two types of bladed hoes in their hands crossed over their chests. Often a seed basket is shown slung by a rope over the back of the figure. In the first millennium BC the ideal number of *shawabti*-figures in a tomb was 365, one for each day of the year. Sometimes figures were dressed in the clothing of the living, carrying whips and staves. These were the overseers, who managed the *shawabti* workers. *Shawabti*-figures were initially made of wood, wax and stone. As greater numbers of figures were employed in the funerary equipment, it became more expedient to make the figures in faience, which could be mass-produced from moulds. The figures could range in material, quality and size. Some were quite cursory. Often the *shawabti*-figures were packed in a wooden box or urn that was then placed in the tomb.

GROUP OF SHAWABTI-FIGURES AND SHAWABTI BOX

Shawabti-figures
Wood, steatite and blue faience
Dimensions: C. 2600: 24,3 x 7,3 x 5,7 cm; C. 2666: 18,4 x 6,5 x 4,5 cm; C. 2806: 25,4 x 9 x 4,6 cm; C. 2509: h 23 cm

Shawabti box (C. 2444)
Painted wood
Dimensions: 32 x 15 x 22 cm

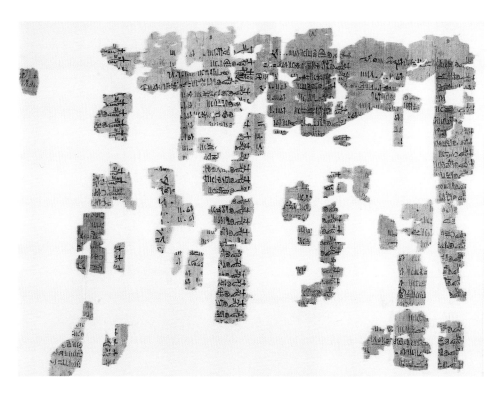

ROYAL PAPYRUS

Papyrus, ink
Dimensions: 183 x 40 cm
New Kingdom, Dynasty XIX (1292-1186 BC)
Provenance: Deir el-Medina, later Drovetti
Collection, 1824
Inv. no. C. 1874 (CGT 54005)

The Frenchman Jean François Champollion deciphered Egyptian hieroglyphs in 1822. Wishing to get first-hand experience of Egyptian sources, he came to Turin in 1824 as the newly acquired Drovetti Collection was being unpacked. He described his excitement at handling the fragments of this papyrus in a letter to his brother. This text, written in cursive hieratic script and arranged in columns, is a list of the kings and their dynasties. Thus, it is one of the most important Egyptian historical documents extant. The text begins from the earliest mythical period and ends with the start of the New Kingdom. Each king's name and the duration of his reign (in years, months and days) appears in each line. The list is subdivided into named groups that do not always coincide with our notion of the dynasties, derived from the later Ptolemaic historian Manetho, who lived in the reign of King Ptolemy II, 282-246 BC. This text was certainly written by a scribe from the workman's village at Deir el-Medina sometime in the Nineteenth Dynasty. The scribe copied it from an official administrative source held in an archive at Thebes. The reverse of the papyrus is inscribed with an administrative text not related to the king-list.

KING RAMESSES II WITH AMUN-RE AND MUT

Red granite
Dimensions: 170 x 113,5 x 94 cm
New Kingdom, Dynasty XIX (1292-1186 BC)
Provenance: Thebes, probably Karnak, later
Drovetti Collection, 1824
Inv. no. C. 767

Grand temple triad sculptures usually depicted a divine family, composed of the god, his consort and their child. Sometimes, as in this case, the image of the king replaced that of the divine child. King Ramesses II sits between the Theban deities Amun and Mut, and their interlocked arms reinforce the idea of divine legitimacy. The equality of size (including the tall crowns) and the reciprocation of the embrace are in stark contrast to the earlier statue group of King Tutankhamun and Amun (see p. 68). Here the king wears ostrich plumes, and a sun disk on ram's horns over a *nemes*-headdress. The ostrich plumes had solar connotations, due to the peculiar dance of this bird at sunrise. Amun wears two falcon tail feathers on his box-like crown, and Mut wears the cow's horns and sun disk, typical of Hathor. The height of the crowns necessitated a tall back slab, whose surface was put to use for the inscribed titles of each figure. Perhaps the near intractability of this granite and the large size of inclusions prevented the artisans from being too adventurous with the facial features. There is almost no correlation between the iconography of this group statue and the black stone image of Ramesses (see p. 83). Here the faces are idealised, almost to the point of being vapid.

TWO SPHINXES

Sandstone
Dimensions: C. 1408: 135,6 x 95 x 296 cm;
C. 1409: 142 x 89 x 302,5 cm
New Kingdom, Dynasty XIX-XX
(about 1250-1145 BC)
Provenance: Karnak, probably Temple of
Khonsu, later Drovetti Collection, 1824
Inv. nos. C. 1408, C. 1409

The Egyptian sphinx, composed of a lion's
body with a man's head (with or without a
straight beard), was a symbolic representation
of the king. Usually the sphinx was shown
recumbent, its royal head adorned with the
nemes-headdress. An alley of sphinx statues
was often used as a route for processions in
front of temples, mostly those connected with
solar deities such as Amun-Re, Re-Harakhte.
Sometimes such rows of sphinxes linked one
chapel to another.

The Turin pair of sphinxes is massive,
measuring some three metres in length, and
they clearly display the stylistic features of
the Ramesside Period. Both have broad faces
with fleshy cheeks, creased eyelids, and a small
mouth with thick lips. The furrows either side

of the mouth and the pierced earlobes are also
typical of the period. The inscriptions do not
name the pharaoh who commissioned them,
but this pair of sphinxes is thought to date from
the reign of King Ramesses III.

A RETROSPECTIVE PORTRAIT OF KING AMENHOTEP I

Painted limestone
Dimensions: 65 x 27 x 40 cm
New Kingdom, Dynasty XIX (about 1250 BC)
Provenance: Deir el-Medina, later
Drovetti Collection, 1824
Inv. no. C. 1372

Although it was King Ahmose who
consolidated the Egyptian empire and founded
the Eighteenth Dynasty and thus the New
Kingdom, it was his son Amenhotep I (1545-
1525 BC), who was venerated for centuries
rather than his father. This was perhaps due
to his sponsorship of architectural projects,
such as the remarkable alabaster chapel at
Karnak dedicated to 'Amun, Enduring of
Monuments'. It was in the 12th century BC,
during the Ramesside Nineteenth Dynasty,
when the artisans' village at Deir el-Medina
flourished, that this retrospective portrait of

King Amenhotep I was made. The choice of white limestone was no doubt intended as an imitation of Egyptian alabaster, a material also used for the King's 'Alabaster Chapel'. The yellow colour of the stripes of the *nemes* headdress and the cartouches was probably meant to represent gold leaf. The King is shown with a ritual beard that is secured by a black chin strap. These straight beards (as opposed to the plaited and curled beard of the god Osiris) were worn by the king when performing his religious duties in the temple.

To the uninitiated, much Egyptian art may look undifferentiated, but here the round face with fleshy cheeks, long nose and small mouth are greatly resemble the features of the black stone sculpture of King Ramesses II. The lidded eyes are, however, sculpted here in shallow orbits. Pierced earlobes were certainly not indicated on royal male figures during the true reign of Amenhotep I, but were an artistic innovation of the Amarna Period. The inscribed epithet 'Lord of the Crown' was a common one in the Ramesside Period and was not current at the beginning of the Eighteenth Dynasty, when King Amenhotep I was alive. This king was venerated as an oracular god by the artisans who built and decorated the royal tombs in the western Theban necropolis. The statue of King Amenhotep I was known to have been carried in procession, and its movements were interpreted as oracles by the priests.

STELE OF KING AMENHOTEP I AND HIS MOTHER AHMOSE NEFERTARI

Painted limestone
Dimensions: 30 x 20 x 3 cm
New Kingdom, Dynasty XIX (1292-1186 BC)
Provenance: Deir el-Medina, later Drovetti Collection, 1824
Inv. no. C. 1452 (CGT 50034)

The veneration of King Amenhotep I often included his mother Ahmose Nefertari, who probably survived her husband Ahmose and may have served as regent for her son. This matriarch is often depicted with black skin, unlike her son, who is normally shown with red skin. On this rounded stele the king and the queen mother, shown with black skin, are represented in the top register in sunk relief. A sun disk ornamented with uraeus-cobras is positioned off-centre over the head of the king. Two votaries, Amenemope the father and Amenemhat his son, kneel and raise their arms in a gesture of praise in the register below. The tall and narrow form of an Egyptian stele dictated the positioning of the figures in order of importance from the top down. Thus the votaries are meant to be seen as worshipping the royal couple above.

The opposite face of the stele depicts an outline sketch of the vizier Hori bearing an ostrich plume, demonstrating that the stele was reused a century later, although probably only for practice by artisans under training.

TWO STATUETTES OF THE DEIFIED QUEEN AHMOSE NEFERTARI

Painted wood
Dimensions: S. 6128: 43 x 9 x 24 cm;
C. 1388: 40,5 x 12 x 12,8 cm
New Kingdom, Dynasty XIX
(1292-1186 BC)
Provenance: S. 6128: Deir el-Medina,
Schiaparelli excavations, 1905;

C. 1388: early acquisition
Inv. nos. S. 6128, C. 1388

Ancient Egyptians, in parallel with more formal veneration in the temples, also worshipped their gods in a private way, utilizing small niches or chapels in their homes. Wooden images were preferred because they were more easily made, albeit of less durable material than stone. Wooden figures could be quite lifelike, because

they did not require a back pillar and the 'webbing' between the torso and limbs as in stone sculpture. Components were sculpted separately and then added for a more natural effect.

Queen Ahmose Nefertari is shown as a youthful woman wearing a figure-hugging, ankle-length, dress. One of the figures shows her with a black face, though the arms and feet are not darkened. This suggests that there is an iconographic motive underlying her colouring and not a genetic one. In each case one arm is raised to the midriff, perhaps to hold a lily sceptre that is now lost. One arm hangs at her side in both statues in order to hold the *ankh*-symbol of life. Over her long tresses she wears a gold-coloured vulture headdress of deified queens, and the modius crown. The figure with the black-painted face was dedicated on behalf of the deceased man Any.

STELE OF NEBRA

Painted limestone
Dimensions: 14,2 x 9,2 x 2,5 cm
New Kingdom, Dynasty XIX
(1292-1186 BC)
Provenance: Deir el-Medina, later
Drovetti Collection, 1824
Inv. no. C. 1591

Just as some Christians address their prayers to saints, so too ancient Egyptians invoked a number of household gods and lesser deities. The village of Deir el-Medina is an exceptional settlement because of the artisans who lived there, who left many enduring monuments, some of which were small but also of great artistic merit. This small stele was dedicated by the draughtsman Nebra, who is not represented himself, though his two sons, Nakhtamon and Khai, also draughtsmen are shown. In the top register, the swallow, symbol of the goddess Menet, is depicted on an altar with a splayed cavetto cornice, before an offering table. The swallow was a bird connected with rebirth, and appears as such in Chapter 86 of the *Book of the Dead*. The cat Tamit appears in the register below. The two young men kneel before her, each with an arm raised in a gesture of adoration. Both the swallow Menet and the cat Tamit appear on other votive monuments in domestic contexts. Cats were frequently kept as pets in ancient Egypt, and could be represented under their master's chair in tomb paintings. The man Nebra and his family are attested in tomb paintings and on other stelae.

HEAR USERSATET'S PRAYER

Limestone
Dimensions: 17 x 14 x 4,5 cm
New Kingdom, Dynasty XIX
(1292-1186 BC)
Provenance: probably Deir el-Medina, later
Drovetti Collection, 1824
Inv. no. C. 1546

Egyptian stelae are rectangular or round-topped, and the top register regularly depicts the deity to whom they are dedicated, often under a sun disk. Stelae can be funerary, intended to venerate the dead, represented in the presence of the deities of the necropolis or in the Netherworld, or they can be also votive, and therefore consecrated in the name of the dedicator during his lifetime. In this case, the man Usersatet (whose theophoric name alludes to the moon goddess Satet) has chosen a peculiar format and iconography for a stele he had made for himself while still alive. The deity to whom he dedicated this small monument is a minor snake goddess, Nebethetepet, Mistress of the Sky. She is not depicted, simply invoked, in a column of hieroglyphic text running down the centre of the stele. Two pairs of human ears, facing left and right, flank the inscription. The lobes of the ears are clearly pierced, and this allows us to date the stele to the post-Amarna period. The fact that the sets of ears appear twice implies that Usersatet wished visually to reinforce the idea of invoking the goddess to 'hear his prayer'. In addition, the ears form a visual pun on the epithet of Nebethetepet, 'the one who hears prayers'. The stele does not contain an actual request, but simply the names of the goddess and dedicator.

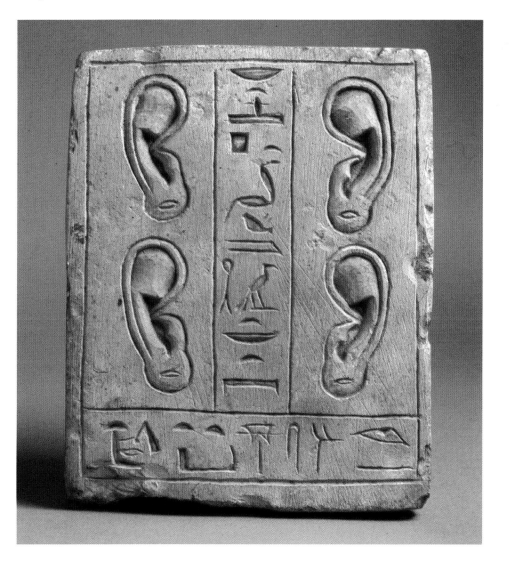

THE GODDESS TAWERET

Painted wood
Dimensions: 40 x 17 x 21 cm
New Kingdom, Dynasty XIX
(1292-1186 BC)
Provenance: Deir el-Medina, later Drovetti
Collection, 1824
Inv. no. C. 526

We have already encountered the hybrid pregnant hippopotamus goddess with legs of a lion and the tail of a crocodile (see p.63). This wooden figurine has the head of a hippopotamus, adorned with a long wig that hangs all the way down to the pendent post-natal breasts. Taweret, whose name means 'the great one', did not have a specific cult site, but as she shared birthing and mothering traits with Hathor, she was often represented in temples of Hathor. According to myth, Taweret grasped the crocodile Seth so that Horus could slay it. Perhaps this accounts for the occurence of Taweret amulets worn by children in order to protect them from encounters with snakes and crocodiles.

As a goddess of marriage and protector of women, especially in childbirth, one would expect this wooden statuette to have been dedicated by a woman. Instead, the text on the base names the man Parahotep, a scribe and draughtsman at Deir el-Medina, and his two sons.

KING RAMESSES II

Tonalite
Dimensions: 196 x 70 x 105 cm
New Kingdom, Dynasty XIX, reign of
Ramesses II (1279-1213 BC)
Provenance: Thebes, later Drovetti
Collection, 1824
Inv. no. C. 1380

This masterpiece in Turin is an arresting image of one of Egypt's longest reigning and most famous pharaohs, King Ramesses II. He wears the Blue Crown or war helmet, and holds the *heqa*-sceptre to his chest. Despite these symbols of power, the great military king in this representations wears a long robe that is draped to create an enormous bell sleeve, and he wears sandals on his feet. Such comfortable clothing shown on sculpture

was an artistic innovation of the Amarna Period, as was the case with realistically modelled features and pierced earlobes. In this sculpture the king's face has sockets for the eyes and eyelids, although the eyebrows and rims are more traditionally incised. The cheeks are fleshy and the nose is long and acquiline, whereas the mouth is small in proportion and turns up at the corners in a benign smile. The chin is small and recessive, creating two furrows running from the corners of the mouth. Remarkably, the king's neck is incised with 'Venus ring' creases.

Modelled in high relief alongside the king's legs are the figures of his chief wife Queen Nefertari, 'Beloved of the Theban goddess Mut', and his son the plume bearer Amonherkhepeshef. Nine bows, signifying the foreign enemies to be symbolically vanquished, are incised under the king's feet. The concept of the king's supremacy is further reinforced by the figures of bound Asian and Nubian prisoners on the front of the base.

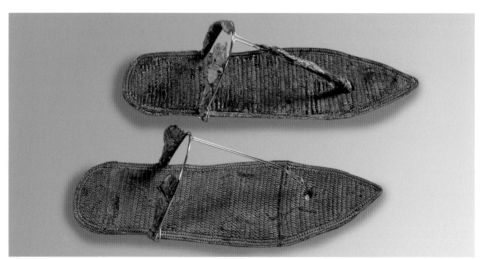

THE TOMB OF QUEEN NEFERTARI

Sarcophagus lid (S. 5153)
Granite
Dimensions: 265 x 110 x 40 cm

Shawabti-figures (S. 5164/5197)
Wood
Height range: 19 cm

Sandals (S. 5160)
Organic fibres
Dimensions: 29 x 10 cm

Wooden coffer lids (S. 5199, S. 5198)
Wood (sycamore)
Dimensions: 13,5 x 9,5 cm; 26 x 19 cm

Djed-pillar, inlaid (S. 5163)
Wood, glass
Dimensions: 15 x 5,5 x 1 cm

Pommel of a sceptre for King Ay (S. 5162)
Limestone and faience
Dimensions: diameter 8 cm

New Kingdom, Dynasty XIX, reign of
Ramesses II (1279-1213 BC)
Provenance: Valley of the Queens / Tomb of
Queen Nefertari (QV 66)
Inv. nos. S. 5153, S. 5164, S. 5197, S. 5154,
S. 5199, S. 5198, S. 5163, S. 5162

In 1904, the Museo Egizio's director Ernesto
Schiaparelli excavated the tomb of Queen
Nefertari (QV 66), wife of King Ramesses II.
The tomb had already been robbed, but
a number of fragmentary objects were
recovered. Pieces of the monolithic granite
lid of the sarcophagus, for example, was
brought to Turin, as were thirty-four
shawabti-figures inscribed for the Queen. A
pair of mummified human knees were also
found, possibly those of Nefertari, along
with a pair of fibre sandals. In addition there
were ceramic and fragmentary stone vessels,
two wooden lids from small coffers (not
found), three wooden *djed*-pillars, possibly
from a bed, a small wooden *djed*-amulet,
inlaid with blue glass and gilded, a wooden
ibis bird, two wooden tails from Anubis
jackal figures and some fragments of cloth.
Similar material was found in the royal tomb
of Tutankhamun. Remarkably, an heirloom
also emerged from the tomb, a faience
pommel from a sceptre with the name of
King Ay, successor of Tutankhamun.

Schiaparelli thoughtfully arranged for
a small-scale model of the elaborately
decorated tomb to be made at the time of its
discovery. This reproduction has attracted
thousands of visitors ever since. It was even
examined by the conservators from the Getty
Foundation before they restored the exquisite
tomb paintings to their former glory.

TWO PROTOMES OF A DEIFIED QUEEN

Wood
Dimensions: Provv. 405: 22 x 13 cm;
Provv. 406: 19,5 x 10,5 cm
New Kingdom, Dynasty XIX
(1292-1186 BC)
Provenance unknown
Inv. nos. Provv. 405-406

Although nothing from ancient Egypt exists in a vacuum, much remains unexplained. These two protome heads evidently represent a deified queen. The vulture headdress, the modius, and the hole for a *uraeus*-cobra at the top of the forehead, tell us as much. However, these long and narrow carvings were certainly not intended as sculptures, but rather as a kind of end-piece that was set on top of a column-like structure or standard.
The shape of the faces with wide cheeks tapering to a small mouth with fleshy lips, lidded eyes, the 'Venus rings' painted on the neck and the presence of pierced earlobes date these features to the Ramesside Period. Due to the intense veneration of Ahmose Nefertari in this period it is possible to hypothesize that these protomes were used in her cult. It is not clear in what way, however. Given that many of her images show her with black skin, it is surprising that these protomes do not have a black complexion. It is to be hoped that future discoveries will unlock the iconographic code to such objects.

LADY HEL

Limestone
Dimensions: 115 x 52 x 35 cm
New Kingdom, Dynasty XIX, reign of
Ramesses II (1279-1213 BC)
Provenance unknown, later Drovetti
Collection, 1824
Inv. no. C. 7352

Wearing a long and elaborate wig of wavy
tresses plaited at the ends, the Lady Hel is
the epitomy of a Ramesside beauty. The
shape of her face with its wide fleshy cheeks
and shallow eye sockets, and the 'Venus ring'
creases on her neck, are all features that we
have seen on Ramesside sculptures. Hel is
completely enveloped by her dress, on which
were probably painted the details of a broad
collar. Traces of red pigment are still evident
on her lips. Essentially, all sculptural detail
was reserved for the wig, whose hairstyle
relates to the real human hair wig found in
the tomb of Kha and Merit (see p.53). Thus,
the wig is centrally parted and the crimped

tresses are plaited at the ends. Two long
plaits either side of the face keep the hair out
of the eyes. A stylised lotus is carved over the
central parting, a detail that often appears
painted on female mummy masks.

Lady Hel holds a *menat*-counterpoise in her
hand across her waist. This cult object was
originally a keyhole-shaped weight that was
worn at the back of the neck, connected to
a beaded collar. Its original purpose was to
balance the many-stranded beaded necklaces
and enable them to hang correctly. Women
took them off and shook them in order to
make a percussive rhythmical sound during
temple rituals. The *menat* was normally
associated with the goddess Hathor's cult.
It was not an object that male priests used,
but was reserved for priestesses. However,
the king is often shown on temple walls
presenting the *menat* to female goddesses.
Lady Hel holds an unidentified rolled-up
object in her left hand on her lap. The
inscription does not help us to further
identify her.

THE DEDICATOR PENCHENABU

Painted limestone
Dimensions: 63 x 20,3 x 46,5 cm
New Kingdom, Dynasty XIX, reign of
Ramesses II (1279-1213 BC)
Provenance: probably Thebes, later Drovetti
Collection, 1824
Inv. no. C. 3032

This votive figure represents the artisan
Penchenabu, who lived in the artisans' village at
Deir el-Medina on the western bank of the Nile
at Thebes, near the Valley of the Kings. He is
shown kneeling to offer an altar surmounted by
the head of a ram, symbol of the god Amun-Re,
a solar version of Amun. The votary has a two-
layered wig, striated at the top and plaited below,
and a short beard, and is wearing a finely pleated
long skirt. His skin is white rather than red,
perhaps to imitate the more precious Egyptian
alabaster (travertine). The figures of Amun and
the deified Ahmose-Nefertari are depicted on
the right and left shoulders in turquoise blue, as
if tattooed on the skin. Tattoos are represented
on other Egyptian objects.

The ram's head protome is painted black on
the horns, woolly hair and beard, whereas the
face and ears are painted yellow to suggest the
golden skin of the god. The inscription in sunk
relief, filled with blue, dates Penchenabu to the
reign of Ramesses II, and was therefore carved
at the same time as the retrospective portrait of
Amenhotep I. This sculpture was acquired from
Drovetti in 1824, but Penchenabu's tomb was
first identified and excavated at Deir el-Medina
(TT 322) a century later.

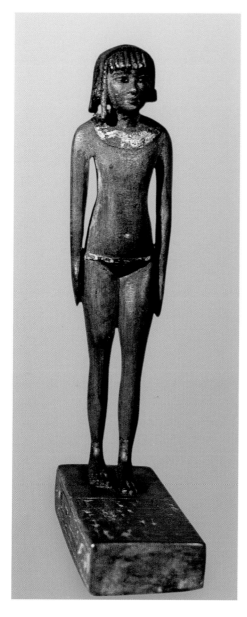

FIGURES OF CHILDREN

Boy (C. 3093)
Painted limestone
Dimensions: 16,6 x 5,5 x 11,6 cm

Girl (C. 3107)
Wood
Dimensions: 20,5 x 4,5 x 11,3 cm

New Kingdom, Dynasty XIX (?), 13th
century BC
Provenance: Theban area, later Drovetti
Collection, 1824
Inv. nos. C. 3093, C. 3107

Few sculptured images of children survive from
Egypt. The most common way of representing
them was as minor figures in the wall
decorations of tombs, often clinging to the leg
of a parent or standing nearby. Usually young
children were represented naked, with the same
proportions and using the same conventions
as adults, but on a smaller scale. Pre-adolescent
boys and girls can be identified by their shaved
heads, and having a long side-lock. Another
iconographic characteristic was the depiction
of the child with an index finger raised to the
mouth, as if it had just been sucked. The god
Horus or Harpokrates could also be depicted as
a child with a side-lock, with his finger raised to
his mouth, to emphasize his descent from Isis.
This small limestone figure of a naked boy
with a side-lock is identified in the funerary
inscription as Amenmes. He wears only a wide
collar and is seated on a high-backed throne
with both hands flat on his lap. The fact that
his finger is not raised to his mouth may
mean that he is somewhat older, possibly an
adolescent. The wooden figure of the standing
girl is Nefertmaau, who like Amenmes is nude,
but has a more mature and developed fringed
hair style that includes a side-lock. She wears a
wide white collar and a thin girdle at her hips
that may allude to her budding adulthood. It is
possible that these figures were commissioned
to commemorate the lives of children who died
before reaching adulthood.

PENBUY AS A STANDARD BEARER

Wood
Dimensions: 61 x 14 x 33 cm
New Kingdom, Dynasty XIX, reign of
Ramesses II (1279-1213 BC)
Provenance: Deir el-Medina, later Drovetti
Collection, 1824
Inv. no. C. 3048

If more expensive, durable and labour-intensive stone was essentially used for royal commissions, then wood and soft limestone were the materials used for the majority of private statues. Various iconographic possibilities were current in the late New Kingdom: the votary could be represented as offering a stele (*stelophoros*) or a shrine (*naophoros*), or, as in this wooden statue, a standard-bearer. These small-scale sculptures were usually placed in chapels or in niches in order to assure a direct and more intimate relation between the dedicator and the god.

Penbuy lived in the artisans' village of Deir el-Medina during the reign of King Ramesses II. This wooden image depicts him wearing a long, elaborately plaited and double-layered wig and a long pleated skirt with a fringe. Penbuy's body is 'framed' by the two tall standards that he is carrying, level with the top of his head. The seated figure of the god Ptah, wearing a sheath garment and holding a *was*-sceptre, sits on top of the standard on his right. He was the patron of craftsmen. His image is also tattooed on Penbuy's right shoulder. The partially preserved figure of the solar god Amun-Re is represented on the standard on his left. A small-scale image of Penbuy's wife, probably the one who dedicated the sculpture for her husband, is incised on the side of the statue in the space left by the advanced left leg.

PENDUA AND HIS WIFE NEFERTARI

Limestone
Dimensions: 78 x 47 x 42 cm
New Kingdom, Dynasty XIX, reign of
Ramesses II (1279-1213 BC)
Provenance: Schiaparelli excavations,
Deir el-Medina, 1905
Inv. no. S. 6127

It was possible for the king to be represented
in a group sculpture with a deity, whereas
private persons could only be shown in the
company of other mortals, which in normal
circumstances meant their family. Pendua
and his wife Nefertari are depicted here on
the same scale in this limestone statue, seated
on a wide, high-backed seat with their arms
passing behind one another so that their
hands rest on each other's shoulders. In
comparison with the earlier royal example
of King Haremhab and his wife (see p.69),

the position of the figures is inverted. A
miniature sunk-relief image of a daughter,
shown smelling a lotus, is depicted on the
back slab between her parents.
Both Pendua and Nefertari, whose name
was the same as the reigning queen, wear
stylish wigs and garments typical of the
period. The thicker plaits framing Nefertari's
face are also found in the real wig of Merit
from the tomb of Kha (see p.53) and on the
sculpture of the Lady Hel (see p.89). Indeed
this couple lived at roughly the same time as
Hel and Penbuy (see p.93). The fact that all
but the wigs and faces are summarily carved
may suggest that the sculpture was hurriedly
finished with the addition of black pigment
to the wigs. An inscription on the back slab
addresses a number of deities, including
Amun-Re, Mut, Khonsu, Atum and Osiris.
The text mentions the names of all the sons
and daughters of the couple, one of whom
appears on another stele in Turin.

KASA'S SHRINE

Painted wood
Dimensions: 33 x 14,5 x 33 cm
New Kingdom, Dynasty XIX, reign of
King Ramesses II (1279-1213 BC)
Provenance: probably Deir el-Medina, later
Drovetti Collection, 1824
Inv. no. C. 2446

The average Egyptian did not have access
to the interior of the temples, as they were
reserved for the priests, who were purified
males, completely clean shaven. Egyptians
were, however, able to view occasional
processions on feast days when the image
or bark of the god's statue was borne
outside the sanctuary and taken to 'visit'
his divine consort at another sanctuary.

This small wooden chapel mirrors the
shape of the chapels or inner sanctums
of temples, where the image of the deity
positioned. Every day the priests opened,
washed, adorned, fed and generally
attended to the statue of the deity. So too
the man Kasa, who owned this small chapel
dedicated to Anukis and by extension
to her divine parents Khnum and Satet,

the triad of the First Cataract region,
attended to the images within. There are
two internal chambers. This small portable
chapel is decorated with the customary
cavetto moulding imitating the splayed
palms of early architecture. On the top
register, the left side of the chapel depicts
Kasa and his wife making offerings to the
divine triad, with the rest of the family
below. On the right side Anukis is pictured
in her shrine on a bark, above a row of
boatmen and other men making libations
on the river bank. More family members
are seen on the bottom register.

Satet and Anukis protected the Nile, and
the ram Khnum controlled the flood waters
of the Nile at Elephantine, its supposed
source, and marked out land for cultivation
with his measuring rope. It is not clear
why Kasa, who lived in Deir el-Medina,
venerated the gods of Elephantine, unless
perhaps his family came from that town, or
he had witnessed a memorable procession
there.

SKETCH OF A DANCER

Painted limestone
Dimensions: 11,5 x 17 x 4 cm
New Kingdom, Dynasty XIX
(about 1200 BC)
Provenance unknown, possibly
Deir el-Medina, later Drovetti Collection,
1824
Inv. no. C. 7052

Ceramic sherds and flakes of limestone
(ostraca) were often used as a medium
for private documents instead of papyrus,
which was expensive. All types of contracts
that might include the hire of a donkey
or receipts for the payment of taxes, for
the recording of stories, for letters, writing
exercises and even sketches were normally
drawn in ink on fragments of pottery
and limestone. These ostraca, frequently
discarded in antiquity, provide an invaluable
insight into Egyptian daily life.

Female images in a non-sacred context
may involve dancing or banqueting, but
are seldom shown naked or displaying

great physical abandon. The ostracon of
a dancer in the Museo Egizio is famous
for all the conventions that it defies. The
lady is naked from the waist up, wearing
only a black sarong with white geometric
patterns (probably batik), wrapped around
her waist. Her only other adornment is a
gold hoop earring that defies gravity. She
is doing a back bend with her shoulders
in profile, as her copious wavy hair hangs
free. The subject is unique in Egyptian
art, but demonstrates clearly that skilled
draughtsmen were capable of producing
images that were 'active' rather than figures
that adhered to the artistic canon: the usual
unnatural rotation of axes (shoulders viewed
from the front, face and limbs in profile).
This semi-erotic sketch, possibly made by a
skilled artisan for his own enjoyment, may
have come from Deir el-Medina.

COLOSSAL FIGURE OF KING SETY II

Red sandstone.
Dimensions: 516 x 113 x 165 cm
New Kingdom, Dynasty XIX,
reign of Sety II (1200-1194 BC)
Provenance: Temple of Karnak, Thebes, later
Drovetti Collection, 1824
Inv. no. C. 1383

The monolithic sandstone figure of King
Sety II was part of a pair originally set up
at the entrance to the small temple that this
pharaoh built to the god Amun in the first
courtyard of the Karnak sanctuary. The
other statue of the pair is now in the Louvre
Museum in Paris.

Sety wears a short wig and a tall, elaborate
and composite crown: an *atef* rush headdress
with ram's horns surmounts the so-called
'Red Crown', symbol of Lower Egypt.
Uraeus-cobras, sun disks and feathers adorn
this complicated headgear. The king wears
a knee-length skirt, whose drop panel is
decorated with a panther head, edged by a
frieze of *uraeus*-cobras. The figure of the god
Amun once stood on top of the standard
carried by Sety.

Given the great importance that the
Egyptians attached to the commemoration
of their names, it is understandable that the
king's titles should appear in several strategic
places: on the base, back-pillar, drop panel
of the skirt and belt and along the standard,
as well as on a small cylindrical boss in his
right hand. The boss was the only way the
Egyptian sculptors could emblematically
represent a staff held horizontally, avoiding
its breakage. Part of the text removed from
the base probably included the name of
the god Seth, used to compose one of the
king's names, a deity that later had negative
connotations. A more recent inscription
states that this colossal statue was found by
Drovetti at Thebes in 1818.

THE SNAKE GODDESS MERETSEGER

Painted limestone
Height: 39 cm
New Kingdom, Dynasty XIX-XX,
(13th-12th century BC)
Provenance: probably Deir el-Medina, later
Drovetti Collection, 1824
Inv. no. C. 957

Meretseger, a snake goddess whose name means 'she who loves silence', personified the Theban necropolis where she dwelt.

Perhaps it was the daily peril of encountering a snake as the artisans worked that led them to respect and venerate her. This statuette is a rare representation in sculpture of this minor deity, who is normally depicted in two dimensions on stelae. This figure probably stood in a chapel of a private nature. Not having been officially excavated, but knowing where Drovetti searched, it is inferred that the piece came from Deir el-Medina, where the tomb workers lived. Indeed, a number of references to this deity occur there.

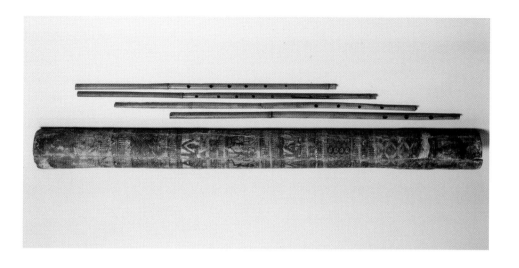

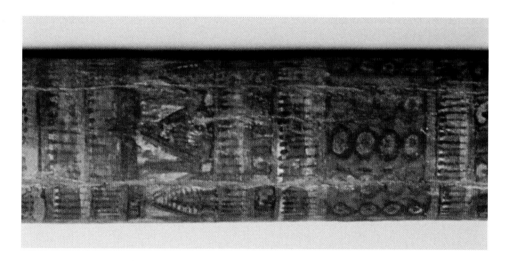

MUSIC MAKING

Flutes
Dimensions: C. 6259/1: 59 cm;
S. 7589: 17 cm; S. 9939: 61 cm;
S. 9940: 42 cm

Painted wooden tubular case (C. 6278)
Dimensions: 70,5 x 6 cm

Date: New Kingdom, Dynasty XIX
(1292-1186 BC)
Provenance: Thebes, necropolis?
Inv. nos. C. 6278, C. 6259/1, S. 7589,
S. 9939, S. 9940

Several types of musical instrument are
known from ancient Egypt, though few
examples survive. Stringed instruments in
the form of lyres have come down to us, as
have a number of percussion instruments
that include cymbals, clappers and sistra
with metal disks. Wind, brass and even reed
instruments are also known from Egypt.
Famously, Tutankhamun's tomb contained
a trumpet made of silver and another made
of copper alloy. A modern mouthpiece was
applied to the silver trumpet in 1939, but
it shattered on being blown (ancient silver
is brittle). The precious instrument was
restored and was played successfully without
the modern mouthpiece for a BBC broadcast
in 1941.

The four wind instruments in Turin were
made in sections of various lengths, fitted
together and perforated with a different
number of holes (3, 4, 6 and 8). Obviously
these produced different ranges and notes.
A carrying case, made from a wooden
hollow tube, was stuccoed and painted with
geometric patterns and a central scene of
dancers in a papyrus marsh.

EROTIC AND SATIRICAL PAPYRUS

Papyrus, ink
Dimensions: 21 x 260 cm
New Kingdom, Dynasty XX
(1186-1070 BC)
Provenance: Deir el-Medina, later Drovetti
Collection, 1824
Inv. no. C. 2031 (CGT 55001)

Papyrus was an expensive medium, and so flakes of stone (ostraca) were normally used for sketches, practice drawings, and even for secular and administrative texts and contracts. So it is rare for a papyrus to be used as the medium for a series of satirical and erotic scenes. It appears that a draughtsman from the artisans' village at Deir el-Medina acquired a sheet of papyrus on which he drew a number of cartoon-like scenes. In one section composed of twelve scenes, men with enormous phalluses are having intercourse with women, surrounded by helpers and a number of props. A bed, stool and chariot are among the furnishings and musical instruments and vessels appear on the floor and under the beds and chairs. While the men are bald (to convey their age) and have grizzled beards, the women are young and beautiful. In fact one young woman with a bobbed haircut is holding a mirror and applying lipstick, seated on an upturned vessel. A dwarf, a monkey and young girls act as helpers or simply form part of the scene, perhaps emphasising its satirical aspect. Inscriptions in cursive hieratic script provide a commentary and dialogue. Scholars have suggested this is a whorehouse patronised by Theban priests, which would account for the touches of satire.

In another section of the same papyrus animals are depicted on two registers, imitating human activities. A variety of animals appear in a series of unconnected scenes that include a battle, a sacrifice, the taking of a prisoner and music making. Certainly two of the scenes satirize temple decoration. In one, a crocodile standing on a chariot drawn by dogs besieges a walled city populated by cats. This is an allusion to royal military campaigns. In the scene directly above, a donkey is slaughtering an animal, possibly a hare, at an offering altar.

This papyrus tells us something of the imagination of the skilled draughtsman from Deir el-Medina and their view of the Theban establishment.

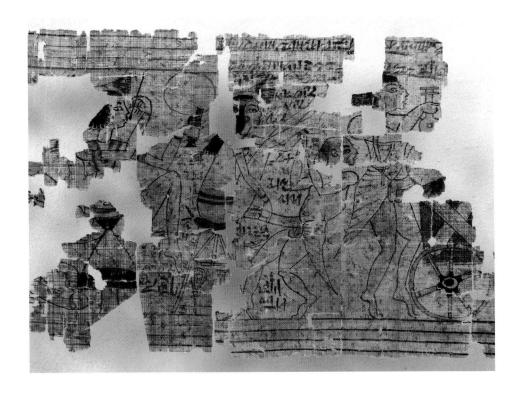

THE KING AND HIS PRISONERS

Sculpture (C. 1392)
Sandstone
Dimensions: 58,5 x 15,3 x 20,5 cm
Provenance unknown, later Drovetti
Collection, 1824

Ostracon (S. 6279)
Limestone
Dimensions: 30,5 x 23 x 3 cm
Provenance: Schiaparelli excavations,
Deir el-Medina, 1905

New Kingdom, Dynasty XX
(1186-1070 BC)
Inv. nos. C. 1392, S. 6279

The Egyptians viewed Egypt as the
cosmos, and the countries outside, which
included Libya, Palestine, Syria and
Nubia, as the chaos of the beyond. These
lands were subdued militarily for strategic
reasons and tribute was demanded. The
foreigner was generically depicted as
an Asian or an African, and often as a
prisoner. Royal iconography involved
representing the king, whose chief role was
to ensure the order of the cosmos (Egypt),
trampling his foes underfoot or killing
them. The external façades of temple
pylons are often carved with scenes of the
king grasping foreigners by a collective
topknot and smiting them with a mace.

This was meant to protect the temple from
possible contamination by foreigners.

The violence of the king's gesture is
moderated in the decoration of the temple
walls, in that he is shown standing upright
in a decorous pose with his mace raised, at
the moment just before the terrible deed,
whereas in this ostracon the draughtsman
depicts the king leaning over to strangle
the unidentified enemy with his bare
hands.

A similar idea is conveyed by the statuette
of the king wearing the rush *atef*-crown
and dragging a bound prisoner by the
hair. The iconography is reinforced by the
presence of a lion (a visual metaphor for
the king) goring the prisoner. Prisoner and
lion are carved in relief against the king's
advanced left leg. The coarse sandstone
was originally plastered and painted.

A MAP OF THE GOLD MINES

Inked and painted papyrus
Dimensions: 41 x 283 cm
New Kingdom, Dynasty XX
(1186-1070 BC)
Provenance: Deir el-Medina, later Drovetti
Collection, 1824
Inv. no. C. 1879

Only a few maps have survived from antiquity, but this kind of document is of extreme interest. On the one hand, such a map allows us to understand the Egyptians' 'geographical' view of the world, and on the other, it enables an approximate location of special structures and settlements.

The renowned Turin map was drawn by the scribe Amennakhte, son of Ipuy, probably in connection with an expedition to the Egyptian Eastern Desert during the reign of King Ramesses IV. The map, more than two metres in length, represents the stony Wadi Hammamat in the Eastern Desert between the Nile and the Red Sea (south is at the top of the papyrus and the eastern road to the Red Sea is on the left). The map has a number of cursive hieratic directions, including the distances, to reach the black *bekhen*-stone (greywacke sandstone)

mountains and the gold mines, situated in the red granite mountains. Different pigments and stylized symbols were also used by Amennakhte to highlight the varied geology of the mountains and to indicate the presence of humans and habitations. The map signals the monumental stele dedicated by King Sety I, a shrine to the god 'Amun of the Pure Mountain', and a village with a water cistern nearby. These places were not continuously inhabited, so the roads needed to be repaired periodically in order to be passable. Although known as the map of the gold mines, because these are indicated along with the locations where the gold was worked, the mines were largely exhausted by this date. In fact, this map was drawn in connection with an expedition to quarry stone for a statue of King Ramesses II to be erected at the Theban Ramesseum.

Amennakhte is a well-attested scribe from the village of Deir el-Medina, whose house and tomb, where a number of other papyri were found, are known. He was also responsible for the plan of the tomb of King Ramesses IV (see p.104).

A PALACE CONSPIRACY

Papyrus
Dimensions: 41 x 540 cm
New Kingdom, Dynasty XX, reign of
Ramesses IV (1152-1145 BC)
Provenance: Deir el-Medina
Inv. no. C. 1875

From time to time information has
come down to us about conspiracies and
assassinations. The reign of Ramesses III was
a time of political instability. Indeed, the
first documented workers' strike is described
in a papyrus in Turin. Another papyrus in
the same museum records in detail a harem
plot to assassinate King Ramesses III. The
conspirators included members of his harem,
one of the king's wives (Tiye, mother of
the pretender Pentaur), priests of Sakhmet
and magicians. The plan involved using
wax figures to disable the guards in a sort of
voodoo, and then kill the king and supplant
the designated heir Ramesses-Hekma-
Meriamun, son of the king's main wife Ese
(Isis), with Pentaur. The magistrates included
overseers of the Treasury, standard-bearers
and royal butlers, known collectively as
'great officials of the Place of Examination'.
It is thought that Ramesses IV ordered the
arrests and trial. Twenty-four people were
found guilty, but it is not known how many
were executed, although we do know that
ten of them were allowed to commit suicide,
including the pretender Pentaur. Some were
punished by having their nose and ears cut
off, and they may have been sent into exile.
Not just the active conspirators but all those
with knowledge of the plot were punished.
Unfortunately, during the trial some of the
judges were found to be involved sexually
with some of the female conspirators, and
they too were severely punished.

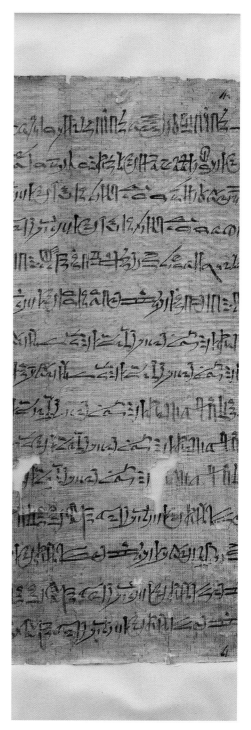

PLAN OF THE TOMB OF KING RAMESSES IV

Papyrus, ink and wash
Dimensions: 35 x 120 cm
New Kingdom, Dynasty XX, reign of
Ramesses IV (1152-1145 BC)
Provenance: Deir el-Medina, later Drovetti
Collection, 1824
Inv. no. C. 1885

As we have seen, the population of the village of Deir el-Medina was essentially composed of men (and their families) working on the royal tombs in the Valleys of the Kings and the Queens. Most were workmen, craftsmen and guards, but there were also scribes, architects and overseers to organize and manage the works. The designs of the tombs were often complex, with many subterranean chambers and walls covered with numerous ritual scenes and texts, that it must have been necessary to draw plans on papyrus prior to the work. Plans of tombs and some superstructures have survived, as have decorative motifs and sketched scenes, although they are very rare.

The scribe Amennakhte, who drew the map of the gold mines and stone quarries of the Wadi Hammamat (see p.102), also made a preliminary plan for the tomb of King Ramesses IV. This drawing includes the measurements, expressed in royal cubits, and closely matches the dimensions of the actual tomb. On the papyrus a cartouche-shaped sarcophagus lid depicts the king flanked by the goddesses Nephtys and Isis inside five rectangles that may indicate gilded wooden shrines, like those in Tutankhamun's tomb. The king's predecessor, Ramesses III, had a similar cartouche-shaped lid with Nephtys and Isis in relief either side of the king, and this now to be found in the Fitzwilliam Museum in Cambridge.

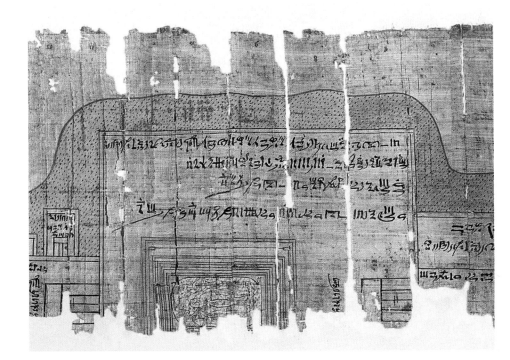

ANTHROPOID SARCOPHAGUS OF BUTEHAMON

Painted and varnished wood
Dimensions: 35 x 120 cm
Third Intermediate Period, Dynasty XXI
(1070-946 BC)
Provenance: TT 291, Thebes, later Drovetti
Collection, 1824
Inv. nos. C. 2236, C. 2237
(CGT 10102, 10103)

Characteristic of the Third Intermediate
Period (first millennium BC) were the richly
painted sarcophagi that seemed to act as a
substitute for decoration of the tomb walls.
Butehamon, the royal scribe of the necropolis,
had two anthropoid coffins with an extra
'false' lid placed directly over the mummy. The
outer coffin is slightly damaged, but many
of its images are reproduced on the inner
coffin. Essentially, the coffins are decorated to
imitate mummy bindings with sacred texts,
processions of deities and other scenes. The
overall yellow tone of the surface is typical
of the Twenty-first Dynasty and is due to
the application of varnish in antiquity. The
creation of the cosmos is depicted on the left

end of each coffin. Geb, the dark-skinned male
god of the earth, lies on the ground with an
erect phallus, while the sky goddess Nut bends
over him, supported by the air god Shu and
other figures on the outer coffin. The most
noticeable difference between outer and inner
coffin is the presence of a large Osiris *djed*-pillar
on the inside of the first coffin, while the
goddess Nut is depicted on the inside of the
inner coffin.

On all the coffin lids, Butehamon wears a long
wig that falls in three lappets, a type that we
have encountered on women, as well as on the
shawabtis of both sexes. On the inner coffin
lids he also has a plaited beard that is curled at
the end and refers to the god Osiris (straight
beards were reserved for the living). On the
inner coffin lids the deceased is also depicted
holding special symbols, the *djed*-amulet
(symbolising Osiris' backbone as well as
the word 'to endure') and the *tyet*-amulet (a
protective knot), while on the 'false' lid of
the mummy he holds two ostrich feathers,
symbolizing righteousness. The underside of
both inner lids is covered with white plaster on
which are inscribed hieratic formulae relating
to the 'Opening of the Mouth' ritual.

BLOCK STATUE OF MERENPTAH

Diorite
Dimensions: 40 x 20 x 27 cm
Late Period, Dynasty XXV, reign of Shabaka
or Shabataka (714-690 BC)
Provenance: Memphis, later Drovetti
Collection, 1824
Inv. no. C. 3063

We have already encountered standing,
striding, seated and kneeling figures, and
now we come to the squatting 'block
statue', an earlier innovation of the Middle
Kingdom (about 2000 BC). The cubic
shape of this statue prevented breakage, as
well as providing a greater surface area for
inscriptions. The block statue was never
used for royal or female images, but only for
private male votive figures.

Merenptah, a priest of the cult of Bastet,
is squatting on the ground with his arms
resting on his knees and his tunic covering
the front of his legs, providing a flat surface
for the inscription. Bastet was a cat goddess
with a cult site in the Delta, whereas the
funerary offering text also invokes Ptah and
other gods of Memphis. In many block
statues the other sides of the figure are flat
planes, but here they reveal the folded nature
of the body. Merenptah wears a bag-shaped
wig that pushes out his ears, an archaising
reference to the earlier Middle Kingdom
style. His face is aged, with flaccid flesh over
a bony structure, and there are carved naso-
labial furrows that are repeated at the corners
of the thin-lipped mouth. His eyes lack
artificial rims and cosmetic stripes.

The near intractability of diorite perhaps
accounts for the clumsiness of the carving,
particularly of the feet and hands. In fact
careful polishing was reserved solely for the
front area of the text, while the rest of the
figure is largely unfinished.

BRONZE GROUP OF DEITIES

Bronze and enamelling
Dimensions: 36 x 6,5 x 15,2 cm
Third Intermediate Period,
Dynasty XXIV-XXV (7th century BC)
Provenance unknown, later Drovetti
Collection, 1824
Inv. no. C. 514

The advantage of bronze was that it allowed the artisans to make elaborate assemblages of figures without the considerable worry of breakage. Here, the goddess Isis stands before a seated image of her spouse Osiris and protectively extends her arms to either side of his plumed crown. The assimilation of Isis with Hathor in the Late Period resulted in the exchange of her original throne crown (the hieroglyph that also spelled her name) for Hathor's usual attributes of cow's horns and sun disk. The composition seems to depict the protection by Isis of an image of Osiris (explaining its smaller scale). The group of statuettes includes a smaller figure of the squatting goddess Maat, who represented truth and cosmic order. The base is decorated with a frieze of *ankh* and *was*-symbols over a *neb*-basket, which can be read as 'all life and power'. The

group used to include a hovering falcon that magically protected the scene, but it has broken off.

The cloisonné cells of the dress of Isis and the sides of the throne of Osiris were inlaid with glass, or more likely filled with enamel. If glass was used, small pieces would have been cut out and glued into the cells. However, it seems that this group was enamelled. Coloured glass powder would have been poured into the cells, and the whole composition would then have been fired in a kiln at a temperature that allowed the glass powder to fuse (around 800° C). The bronze alloy of the group would need be low in lead so that it could withstand the high temperature required for melting glass. Lead was needed for complicated bronze compositions because it helped to push the molten metal into the elaborate moulds, and the lack of it here must have made this group more difficult to produce (as well as accounting for the brittle nature of the metal that resulted in the falcon breaking off), but this was compensated by the colourful enamelling.

THE GODDESS PROTECTING THE SOVEREIGN

Panel of the goddess and the king (C. 518)
Dimensions: 24,5 x 18 x 1 cm

Panel of the snake goddess and the king's cartouche (C. 979)
Dimensions: 17 x 11 x 1 cm

Fretted wood
Late Period, Dynasty XXV-XXVI
(7th century BC) – Ptolemaic Period
(3rd century BC)
Provenance unknown
Inv. nos. C. 518, C. 979

The role of female deities grew in importance in the Late Period at a time when images of mortal women were rare. The two fretted wooden panels depict the protective power of two goddesses. In one case, the goddess Isis is depicted as a woman, but with large wings attached to her arms that are protectively extended towards the king, shown kneeling on a small altar. The cloisonné cells of the imbricated pattern on the wings were once filled with coloured glass. The fact that the panel is flat and not meant to be seen in the round suggests that it was once a kind of decorative openwork frieze, perhaps part of a 'storyboard' sequence attached to a temple or a piece of royal furniture. Another similar panel depicts the cobra goddess Wadjet, also with wings (male deities did not have protective wings), this time protecting not the king but a cartouche with his name. The cartouche signified the realm and eternal cycle of the sun and, as such, always surrounded royal names. This too must once have blazed with colourful glass inlays, of which only a few traces remain. What has not survived is a further panel of the frieze that would have included the vulture goddess Nekhbet extending her wings on the other side of the cartouche. Together Wadjet and Nekhbet were known as the 'Two Ladies', and symbolised Upper and Lower Egypt.

THE BA-SPIRIT

Statuette of a bird with a human head
(C. 6963/4)
Dimensions: 17,7 x 4 x 11,6 cm
Ptolemaic Period, 4th century BC

Round-topped stele (C. 1529)
Dimensions: 42,2 x 29,8 x 2 cm
Roman Period, 1st century AD

Painted wood
Provenance unknown, later Drovetti
Collection, 1824
Inv. nos. C. 6963/4, C. 1529

Despite the emphasis in ancient Egypt on the
preservation of the body, the concept of death
also involved a liberation of the soul from the
body. There was more than one type of soul in
ancient Egypt, but the *ba*-spirit was envisaged
as a bird with a human head that was able to
leave the confines of the tomb and flit around
the necropolis. Indeed, man-made ponds
shaded by sycamore trees were located in the
western cemeteries to provide refreshment for
the *ba*. In some scenes on stelae and sarcophagi
the sycamore goddess emerges from the top of
the tree to pour a liquid libation to the *ba*-bird
who rests in her shade. In rare cases, such as
the present one, the *ba*-spirit is depicted
as a small statuette with a human head
surmounted by the solar disk.

A Roman stele expresses the idea of the soul as
separate from the mummy pictorially. In a kind
of visual narrative, the mummy is presented
by the jackal god of the necropolis, Anubis.
However, the central focus is the *ba*-spirit,
sitting on top of an altar, to which liquid
libations and offerings of incense and bread are
made by the deceased's surviving son.

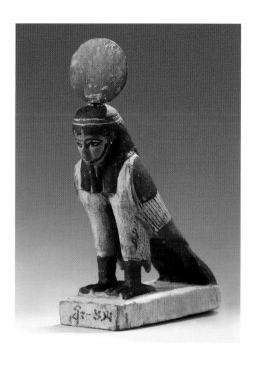

THE GODS ANUBIS, THOTH AND HORUS

Statuette of a jackal, Anubis (C. 914)
Dimensions: 24,3 x 29,4 x 7 cm

Statuette of an ibis, Thoth (C. 1009)
Dimensions: 23,5 x 24 x 8 cm

Statuette of a falcon, Horus (C. 986)
Dimensions: 26,5 x 22 x 8 cm

Painted wood
Ptolemaic Period, 4th century BC
Provenance unknown
Inv. nos. C. 914, C. 1009, C. 986

According to myth, the jackal-headed god Anubis invented the art of embalming and afterwards revealed the secret of conserving the body after death to the Egyptians. For this reason, priests were often depicted wearing a jackal-headed mask in order to give the impression that the god Anubis himself was embalming the corpse. Such scenes are found on a number of painted sarcophagi and a terracotta Anubis mask in the Egyptian collection in Hildesheim, Germany. The Turin wooden jackal figurine is inscribed with the name Wepwawet, or the 'Opener of the Way' here with the additional epithet 'of the North'. The fact that it has a rectangular piece cut out of the base suggests that it was once mounted on a standard and held aloft in the funerary procession of the man Nespatawy, son of Osoreris, priest and prophet of the god Min.

Two other figurines from standards come from the same man's tomb. A figure of the ibis deity Thoth, god of wisdom and writing, was also appropriate as he was the patron of scribes. His reckoning abilities resulted in his taking the role of scribe on the day of judgement, when the deceased's heart was weighed against the 'feather of the goddess Maat' (Truth). The figure of Horus's falcon represented the deity who vanquished Seth, the murderer of the god Osiris, king of the Netherworld. All three figures have hieroglyphic inscriptions on the base, as well as texts in demotic script on the front. Both the falcon and the ibis figurines include a reference to the god Thoth-Apis, a special combination of deities that protects the corpse.

ISIS AND NEPHTYS

Gilded wood
Dimensions: 509/1: 10 x 5,9 cm,
509/2: 10 x 5,8 cm
Late Period, about 6th- 4th century BC
Provenance unknown
Inv. nos. Provv. 509/1-2

According to myth, Isis and Nephtys were
both sisters and sisters-in-law. Isis was the
mother of Horus and wife of Osiris. Her
emblem of the royal throne as a crown was
also the hieroglyph that spelt her name.
Through her act of mourning for her
murdered husband, Isis became associated
with the dead.

Nephtys (with a tall crown topped by a
basket), was the wife of Seth, who had
murdered his brother Osiris. As in a Greek
tragedy, Nephtys proved that blood is
thicker than marriage, and went to the aid
of her sister Isis. Together they gathered the
dismembered body parts of Osiris and saved
the corpse from putrefaction. Thus Nephtys
and Isis, together with Neith (a warrior
goddess) and Selket (a scorpion goddess),
made up the foursome who protected the
dead. They were often represented on the
corners of coffins and each was responsible
for one of the canopic deities whom we will
encounter below (see p.114).

These thin, gilded talismanic figures
resemble hieroglyphs in their simplicity. The
women kneel in profile with their hands
to their faces, a gesture of mourning and
lamentation for the deceased Osiris. By
extension, their image was used for every
deceased man and woman. These figures
were once laid on a mummy and held fast by
the linen bindings.

TOWARDS THE COMFORT OF THE MUMMY

Soles (C. 2330, C. 2331)
Painted and stuccoed linen
Dimensions: 22,5 x 8,3 cm (C. 2330),
20 x 8,5 cm (C. 2331)
Late Period, Dynasties XXV-XXXI
(712-332 BC)
Provenance unknown

Hypocephalus (C. 2324)
Painted and stuccoed linen
Dimensions: diameter 14 cm
Late Period, Dynasties XXV-XXXI
(712-332 BC)
Provenance unknown, later Drovetti
Collection, 1824
Inv. nos. C. 2330, C. 2331, C. 2324

Hypocephali and the soles of sandals were
frequently applied to the bound mummy
in the Late Period. As the term implies, the
hypocephalus was placed under the head, and
is a circular decorated disk, whereas the soles
were meant to represent the underside of the
sandals.

The hypocephalus is usually outlined in black
with a rich solar iconography. The Apis bull
that transported the mummy is inverted in
the bottom row. At the top we see the passage
to the Afterlife by the ba-spirit, represented
as a bird on a solar bark. Another solar
bark precedes it, with a baboon holding the
protective eye of Horus before the seated sun
god Re-Harakhte. A central register shows
baboons standing with their front legs raised
in adoration before the four-headed ram god
Khnum-Re. The peculiar habit that baboons
have of standing on their back legs and raising
their faces to the sun at dawn while making
very excited noises (presumably as they warmed
themselves in its heat), led the Egyptians to
believe that they were praying to the rising sun.
The disk is meant to produce a radiating heat
that warms the mummy. This hypocephalus
belonged to Nes-ta-netjeret-ten.

The depiction of foreigners on the sandal soles,
usually an Asian and a Nubian, was derived
from royal iconography that showed the king
trampling his enemies underfoot, thereby
assuring the integrity of the cosmos or Egypt.
Here the brightly painted Nubian and bearded
Asian are distinguished by their skin colour,
facial features, hairstyles, and garments typical
of their homelands. Both are bound at the
elbows and ankles, with a red and brown rope
respectively.

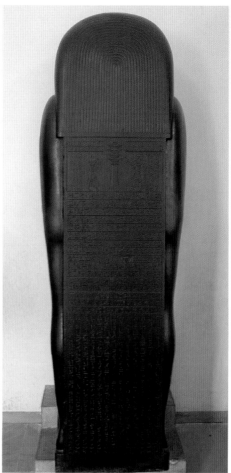

GEMENEFHERBAK'S COFFIN

Meta-greywacke
Dimensions: 228 x 88 x 46 cm
Late Period, Dynasty XXVI (664-525 BC)
Provenance: Sais, later Drovetti Collection, 1824
Inv. no. C. 2201

This basalt anthropoid sarcophagus, dating from the Twenty-sixth Dynasty, belonged to the vizier Gemenefherbak, whose title was the equivalent of a prime minister in the seventh century BC. The initial impression is that the sarcophagus is made of metal and not of stone. Indeed the material is known as metagreywacke, a stone with a metallic sheen. In Egypt it was called *bekhen*-stone, and it was mined in Egypt's eastern desert, in the region of the Wadi Hammamat. It is even noted on the topographical and geological map in the Museum (see p.102).

Gemenefherbak is represented on the

lid wearing a long wig, the plaited and curled divine beard of Osiris, and a large *wesekh*-collar. A small engraved squatting figure of Maat, the deity of justice, is discernible, suspended from a cord around his neck in reference to his role as Chief Justice. The spectator's eye is immediately drawn to the large winged scarab, a symbol of rebirth and regeneration, carved on the chest of the mummiform lid. Its position over the heart, the seat of intelligence, was important and guaranteed its protection. Two columns of engraved funerary offering text are inscribed down the centre of the lid between the subtly modelled knees.
The external underside of the coffin has been admired by thousands of visitors for the beauty of its inscription. Gemenefherbak appears twice in a small scene among finely inscribed hieroglyphs, adoring the *djed*-pillar, sacred to Osiris. The texts identify the deceased and are meant to ensure the provision of sustenance in the Afterlife.

CANOPIC VESSELS
OF WAH-IB-RA

Egyptian alabaster
Dimensions: 36/38 x 15 cm
Late Period, Dynasty XXVI (664-525 BC)
Provenance: possibly Memphis, later
Drovetti Collection, 1824
Inv. nos. C. 3208/1-4 (CGT 19028-19031)

These four vessels once held the internal
organs of the official Wah-ib-ra, who
lived during the Twenty-sixth Dynasty in
the sixth century BC. Removed during
mummification, the stomach, lungs, liver
and intestines were dried in natron and
usually placed in vessels that we refer to
now as canopic jars. These had lids in the
shape of the head of the relevant protective
deity, one of the Four Sons of Horus.
Amset, depicted as a man, protected the
liver and was spiritually connected with the
ka essence of the deceased. The vessel with
a lid in the shape of Hapi, the baboon deity,
contained the deceased's lungs, whereas
Duamutef the jackal protected the stomach

and the *ba*-spirit. Kebehsenef the falcon
looked after the intestines and the sa aspect
of the deceased. The goddess Isis and her
sister Nephtys, along with Nut and Selket,
protected the dead as well, and were often
invoked, as on the canopic vessel here.

Other organs such as the heart were usually
treated and put back into the chest cavity,
whereas the brain was normally discarded.
In the Twenty-First Dynasty embalming
practices made it possible for the organs
once placed in the canopic jars to be
reinserted in the dried body of the deceased.
Indeed, this possibility existed earlier in the
time of Kha, whose tomb was not equipped
with canopic jars. On the other hand, the
canopic jar tradition was so strong that in
some cases fake vessels with lids in the form
of the Sons of Horus were produced. The
canopic jars of Wah-ib-Ra appear to have
been used in antiquity for the purpose that
was originally intended.

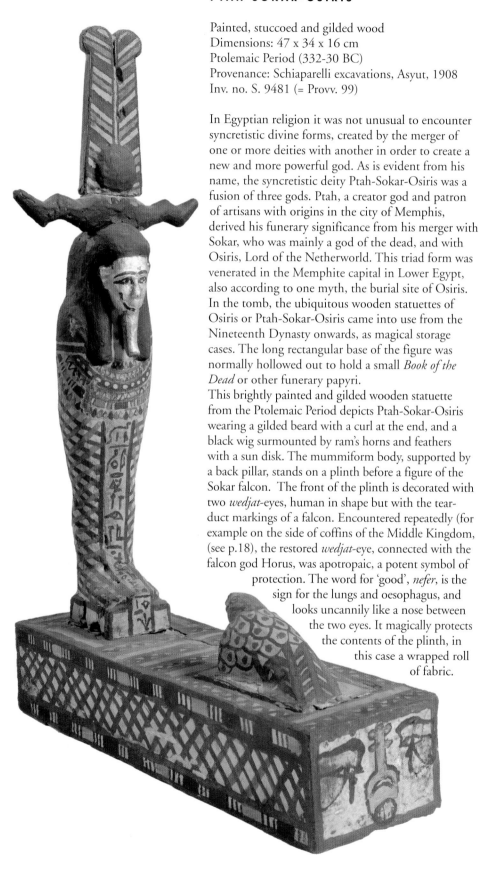

PTAH-SOKAR-OSIRIS

Painted, stuccoed and gilded wood
Dimensions: 47 x 34 x 16 cm
Ptolemaic Period (332-30 BC)
Provenance: Schiaparelli excavations, Asyut, 1908
Inv. no. S. 9481 (= Provv. 99)

In Egyptian religion it was not unusual to encounter
syncretistic divine forms, created by the merger of
one or more deities with another in order to create a
new and more powerful god. As is evident from his
name, the syncretistic deity Ptah-Sokar-Osiris was a
fusion of three gods. Ptah, a creator god and patron
of artisans with origins in the city of Memphis,
derived his funerary significance from his merger with
Sokar, who was mainly a god of the dead, and with
Osiris, Lord of the Netherworld. This triad form was
venerated in the Memphite capital in Lower Egypt,
also according to one myth, the burial site of Osiris.
In the tomb, the ubiquitous wooden statuettes of
Osiris or Ptah-Sokar-Osiris came into use from the
Nineteenth Dynasty onwards, as magical storage
cases. The long rectangular base of the figure was
normally hollowed out to hold a small *Book of the
Dead* or other funerary papyri.

This brightly painted and gilded wooden statuette
from the Ptolemaic Period depicts Ptah-Sokar-Osiris
wearing a gilded beard with a curl at the end, and a
black wig surmounted by ram's horns and feathers
with a sun disk. The mummiform body, supported by
a back pillar, stands on a plinth before a figure of the
Sokar falcon. The front of the plinth is decorated with
two *wedjat*-eyes, human in shape but with the tear-
duct markings of a falcon. Encountered repeatedly (for
example on the side of coffins of the Middle Kingdom,
(see p.18), the restored *wedjat*-eye, connected with the
falcon god Horus, was apotropaic, a potent symbol of
protection. The word for 'good', *nefer*, is the
sign for the lungs and oesophagus, and
looks uncannily like a nose between
the two eyes. It magically protects
the contents of the plinth, in
this case a wrapped roll
of fabric.

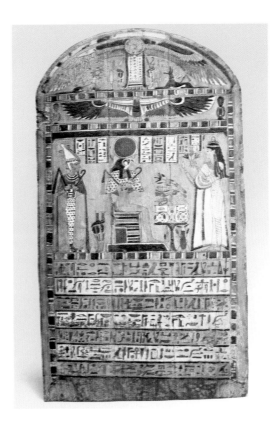

STELE OF NESKHONSU

Painted wood
Dimensions: 58,5 x 33,5 x 3 cm
Ptolemaic Period (about 300 BC)
Provenance: Thebes, acquired before 1888
Inv. no. C. 1597

A stele, whether votive or funerary, rectangular or round-topped, is usually divided into a number of decorated sections with registers of inscribed text. This type of monument was a dedication to Egyptian deities or deceased persons. Nearly everyone (the king, a member of the nobility, an official, or a simple artisan) could dedicate a stele, of differing size and quality, depending on their means, to his or her favourite god in a temple or a small chapel. The texts are often hymns or prayers to the god and usually mention the votary, so that the man or woman (thanks to the presence of his or her name) and the god would be connected for all eternity.

In this funerary stele, the deceased woman Neskhonsu, a musician in the Temple of Amun-Re, is depicted on the right before the gods Re-Harakhte and Osiris. The left side of the stele tended to be the 'divine side'. Thus, if the scene had been made up of the living family making offerings to the deceased the latter would have been positioned on the 'divine side'.

The falcon-headed Re-Harakhte (a fusion of Horus with the sun god) wears a large sun disk and carries the royal flail and crook. The fact that he is enthroned on a *maat* plinth suggests that this is a 'true likeness' of the god, therefore a statue. Osiris stands behind him, in reality to be interpreted as alongside him.

Neskhonsu is dressed in white and wears a perfume cone on her head. Its contents were supposed to melt. She was the daughter of the Amun priest Padiamonnebnesuttauy and the Amun-Re singer Irtyeru. Neskhonsu followed in the footsteps of her deceased mother and acted as singer in the same temple. Appropriately, she offers her musical instrument, the sistrum, and a bouquet of lotus blossoms to the gods. The rounded upper part of the stele is decorated with a winged sun disk provided with *uraeus*-cobras wearing the crowns of Upper and Lower Egyptian, and flanked by the jackal god Anubis. The brightly coloured inscribed prayers invoke the gods to grant bread, beer, meat, wine, milk, incense, scented oils, vessels, clothing and all beautiful things that the deceased will require in the Afterlife.

MAGICAL STATUE

Black granite
Dimensions: 50 x 24,8 x 11,5 cm
Late Dynasty XXX to Early Ptolemaic Period
(4th century BC)
Provenance unknown, later Drovetti
Collection, 1824
Inv. no. C. 3030

Another sculptural innovation of the Late Period was a new kind of stele showing the god Horus as the child Harpokrates, standing on crocodiles holding two groups of dangerous beasts that include serpents, a scorpion and a lion (in his left hand) and serpents, a scorpion and an antelope (in his right hand). The mask-like head of the god Bes is at the top of the stele. This type of stele, called a *Horus cippus*, was a magical and healing monument that was often inscribed with the story telling how Horus was poisoned by his enemies and cured by the prayers of Isis. Here the stele is incorporated into a larger composition that includes a male votive figure presenting it (a *stelophoros*), that is covered with magical texts. The votary is the man Hor, whose head has not survived. The elaborate texts with friezes of magical guardians are not only engraved on his long kilt but cover his exposed arms in a kind of tattoo, as well as on and the back pillar of the statue. Water was poured over the texts and stele, and the magically charged liquid was then used as a medicinal cure that could be drunk or applied to bites and injuries.

SCULPTOR'S MODELS

King's bust (C. 7047)
Limestone
Dimensions: 17 x 13,3 x 9,5 cm

Plaque with Bes (C. 7053)
Sandstone
Dimensions: 13,5 x 11,5 x 3 cm
Provenance unknown

Chick (S. 2893)
Limestone
Dimensions: 17 x 14 x 2,5 cm

The Two Ladies (S. 2898)
Limestone
Dimensions: 16,5 x 20 x 2 cm
Provenance: Heliopolis (Kom)

Late Period, Dynasty XXV-XXXI (712-332 BC)
Inv. nos. C. 7047, C. 7053, S. 2893, S. 2898

Among the immigrants into Egypt during the Ptolemaic Period there were certainly Greek-speaking artisans, who studied the traditional Egyptian styles. This would explain the profusion of works of art that we call 'sculptors' models'. Not infrequently they are only partially worked. These models include relief plaques, along with limestone and plaster royal busts and heads. The plaque is usually a sort of pictorial 'window' that depicts isolated human and animal figures. The fact that most of these plaques appear unfinished, that the remains of a proportional grid are sometimes still visible, and that they lack painted detail, has led scholars to regard these artefacts as models. Some have an inscribed dedication, and this may imply that the plaques and busts were used as a teaching aid or exercise and were dedicated as votive offerings. Many of these 'models' can be dated stylistically to the early Ptolemaic Period, and suggest the presence of foreign artisans who were being inducted into the royal sculpture workshops.

The limestone bust of a king wearing the *nemes*-headdress is typical of this type of partially sculpted model bust. The facial features are nondescript, but datable to the reign of an early Ptolemaic king, perhaps Ptolemy III. Two of the small plaques in raised relief show trial hieroglyphs: a quail chick (the hieroglyph for the sound 'w'), a vulture (for the goddess Nekhbet) and a cobra (for the goddess Wadjet), known as the 'Two Ladies', deities who symbolised Upper and Lower Egypt. The third plaque in sunk relief establishes the experimental nature of such objects. Two heads, one of Bes, a minor deity, the other of the hieroglyph for the human face, appear on the top register, while the owl (for the preposition 'm') and the chick hieroglyphs are on the one below.

A PTOLEMAIC ROYAL HEAD

Basalt
Dimensions: 19 x 16,2 x 14,5 cm
Ptolemaic Period, possibly reign of Ptolemy II
(282-246 BC)
Provenance unknown, later Drovetti
Collection, 1824
Inv. no. C. 1399

After the conquest of Egypt by Alexander the Great, and following his premature death, his general Ptolemy assumed the throne and ushered in the Ptolemaic Dynasty that ruled for some three centuries. Large numbers of Greek speakers from numerous lands migrated to Egypt, with the result that the Greek language came to be used alongside Egyptian. In addition, Egyptian and Hellenistic artistic idioms coexisted during these centuries. The sixteen Macedonian kings of the Ptolemaic Dynasty chose to support the native Egyptian religion, out of their desire to be accepted as real pharaohs. Thus they continued to build temples in the Egyptian style, as well as adding to existing ones. The temples were enriched with statuary in the traditional Egyptian idiom.

This royal head, with the *nemes*-headdress, was probably sculpted by an Egyptian during the first few years of the Ptolemaic Period. Although the rest of the body is lost, the figure would doubtless have been shown in the traditional manner, seated or standing with the left leg advanced and wearing a kilt. Even the uninitiated can recognise the stylistic features of the period: the subtle modelling, the artificial almond-shaped eyes, the soft natural ridge of the eyebrows, the fleshy cheeks, the 'benign smile', and the roughened alternating stripes of the *nemes* headdress. These features are substantially different from those of sculptures of the same period in the Hellenistic idiom, which are familiar to us from coinage.

TWO PTOLEMAIC QUEENS

Sandstone
Dimensions: 102 x 42,5 x 23 cm
Early Ptolemaic Period (4th- 3rd century BC)
Provenance unknown, later Drovetti
Collection, 1824
Inv. no. C. 1386

Basalt
Dimensions: 44 x 26,7 x 21 cm
Late Ptolemaic Period (2nd-1st century BC)
Provenance unknown, later Drovetti
Collection, 1824
Inv. no. C. 1385

Just as the Ptolemaic kings chose to be
represented in the Egyptian as well as the
Hellenistic idiom (better suited to marble),
their queens, all of whom were called Berenice,
Arsinoe or Cleopatra, were portrayed in both
styles.

Although the features of the sandstone figure
are a little battered, this Ptolemaic queen can
be dated to the early years of the Ptolemaic
Dynasty. She wears a long plaited wig that is
held in place by a diadem with a *uraeus*-cobra.
Whereas queens normally wore the vulture

headdress in the New Kingdom, in the
Ptolemaic Period, only dead and deified ones
wore it. Instead of a tunic, this queen has on
a long, clinging and wrap-around pleated
garment. She holds a lily sceptre in her right
hand that emerges from the garment, and the
ankh-symbol of life at her left side. Her arm
is elongated in proportion to the trunk of her
body, a characteristic of the period. Despite the
poorly preserved face, the fleshy cheeks, the
neck and the 'buttonhole' eyes are typical of the
early Ptolemaic Period.

Another sculpture of a Ptolemaic queen in
the Museum has a different iconographic
repertoire. This queen wears a vulture
headdress and three *uraeus*-cobras at the brow.
No garment is detectable, possibly due to the
harder nature of the stone. Her face is fleshy
but her eyes are sunken. Such features could
identify the statue as a late portrait of Queen
Arsinoe II or Berenice II, both of whom were
deified and worshipped until the first century
BC. Since Berenice added Cyrene to Egypt's
possessions, this may account for the presence
of three *uraeus*-cobras, the first two symbolising
Upper and Lower Egypt, and thus the statue
could be attributable to her.

GENERAL PETIMUTHES

Diorite
Dimensions: 121 x 36 x 44 cm
Ptolemaic Period, reigns of Queen
Cleopatra III and Ptolemy X, about 100 BC
Provenance: Temple of Karnak, Thebes,
later Drovetti Collection, 1824
Inv. no. C. 3062

After Alexander the Great's death his vast
empire was divided among his generals:
Ptolemy took over Egypt and Seleucus Syria
(founded in 312 BC). Seleucid dynastic strife
resulted in the break-up of Syria, turning it
into a minor and quarrelsome kingdom that
troubled Egypt and later Rome.
Egypt profited from the dynastic squabble
between Antiochus VIII and his maternal
half-brother Antiochus IX, and attacked
Ptolemais-Akko, a city in present-day
Israel. The victorious Egyptian army was
commanded by Petimuthes, as attested
by his statue set up later in the Temple of
Amun-Re at Karnak. The sculpture, now
headless, depicts the striding general in the
tunic, skirt and wrap-around fringed shawl
of the Persian court, with an obelisk-shaped
back pillar.

When discovered in 1824 both the head and
feet of the sculpture were missing. However,
the feet were recovered almost a century and
a half later in 1970 during an excavation
at Karnak. A cast of this find was added to
the figure, and the texts on it adds further
details of Petimuthes, son of Psenobastis
and Tabaket, born in Tel el-Balamun in the
Delta. He commanded the Egyptian army
during the reign of Cleopatra III. It is hoped
that further excavations will eventually result
in the discovery of the head.

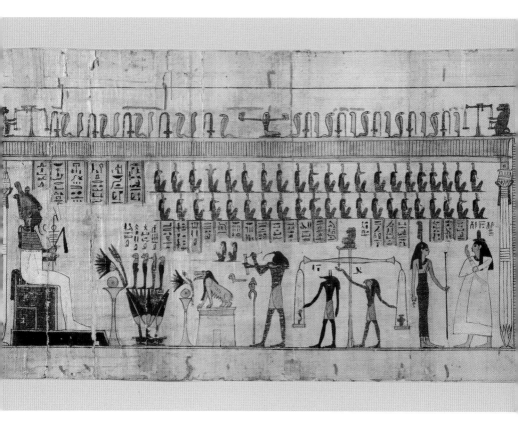

BOOK OF THE DEAD OF TAISNAKHET

Papyrus
Dimensions: 35 x 865 cm
Ptolemaic Period (3rd-1st century BC)
Provenance: Thebes, later Drovetti
Collection, 1824
Inv. no. C. 1833

We have encountered the *Book of the Dead* in the tomb of Kha, but the present one was prepared for a woman named Taisnakhet, who lived almost a thousand years later. The text is a magical one that enabled the deceased to overcome the obstacles and dangers of the passage to the Afterlife.

This scene represents the last judgement, at which the destiny of the soul was determined. The so-called *psychostasis* or weighing of the soul takes place in a chapel before the seated Osiris, with forty-two overseeing deities above. The heart of the deceased (for the Egyptians the heart, and not the brain, was the seat of intelligence) is placed on a balance opposite the feather of the goddess Maat, who represents Truth and Order. The goddess Maat appears opposite the deceased lady Taisnakhet to the right. Anubis and Horus preside over the scene, as does the ibis deity Thoth, who as the god of reckoning pens the result of the tribunal on his scribal palette before the god Osiris. If the heart were to prove heavier than the feather of Truth, a hybrid beast, shown on the small altar, would devour it, thus preventing Taisnakhet from reaching the Afterlife.

THE CHILD PETAMENOPHIS

Mummy (C. 2230/1)
Human remains, linen
Length: 100 cm

Sarcophagus (C. 2230/2-3)
Painted and stuccoed wood
Dimensions: 110 x 40 x 42 cm

Roman Period, Emperor Hadrian
(117-138 AD)
Provenance: Thebes, Khokha / Tomb of
Thutmose (TT 32)
Inv. nos. C. 2230/1, C. 2230/2-3

During the so-called Late Period, there was
an influx of foreigners into Egypt from the
Mediterranean area. Over successive generations
intermarriage and cultural assimilation
took place, with the result that foreigners
adopted Egyptian funerary traditions.
The boy Petamenophis lived at the beginning of
the second century AD, during the reign of the
Roman emperor Hadrian, and died in 123/5 (?)
AD. Despite his Egyptian name, Petamenophis'
parents were probably of Greek origin,
suggested by the funerary inscriptions painted
on the wooden coffin. Even these reflect
the bicultural background of the family: a
hieroglyphic inscription is written in ink on the
lid and there is a Greek text on one of the short
sides. According to the latter, Petamenophis
lived for four years, eight months and ten days.
The mummy is covered with elaborate lozenge-
shaped bindings and rests on a small pillow.
The head of the child is adorned with a plaster
funerary wreath covered in gold leaf. The simple
wooden coffin has a vaulted lid with four small
corner pillars, typical of the period. The inner
decoration of the coffin reveals the remarkable
extent of Graeco-Roman influence on Egyptian
art. The figure of the sky goddess Nut, depicted
frontally rather than in profile, has curly black
hair and goggle eyes. Nut wears contemporary
jewellery: S-shaped hoop earrings, a beaded
necklace with a pendant in the form of a
crescent moon, and a snake bracelet. Her long
multicoloured skirt is a stylised reference to
the earlier feather-patterned dress of goddesses.
Flanking Nut are two kneeling females with
hands raised to their faces, representing the
mourning goddesses Isis and Nephtys, against a
background of tree branches with red berries.

MUMMY PORTRAIT

Encaustic on wooden panel
Dimensions: 41,5 x 13,8 x 1 cm
Roman Period, late 1st early 2nd century AD
Provenance: Antinoë (?), purchased 1974
Inv. no. S. 18177

At about the time that Petamenophis died
(see p.124), a young girl, perhaps with mixed
Greek and Egyptian blood, was prepared
for burial. A panel painted with her portrait
was placed over her face and bound into
the mummy wrappings at the corners. Thus
the deceased was clearly identified. Whereas
the goddess Nut painted on the coffin of
Petamenophis shows Hellenistic details,
she is executed in a flat painted style. This
picture of a young girl, on the other hand,
is painted in a lifelike and stylistically highly
developed manner, with shading of the
orbits, and having the naso-labial furrows
both sides of the heart-shaped mouth, and
fleshy chin. Some of the darkening along
the right side of the face was caused by the
mummy bindings. The girl's large eyes, set
in deep sockets under thick black eyebrows
that join over the nose, are characteristic of
Hellenistic and Roman portraits.

Many such panels were discovered in the
nineteenth century, mainly in the Faiyum
area. They were subsequently detached from
the mummy bindings and sold to European
collections. Some of these so-called Faiyum
portrait panels are inscribed with Egyptian
or Greek names (written in demotic
Egyptian or Greek), including theophoric
examples (incorporating the names of both
Egyptian and Greek deities, such as Isidoros,
Artemidoros).

This bust-length panel of an unmarried
girl (she is not veiled and her hair is tied
back) is painted in 'encaustic' technique,
which involves heating pigment in wax
and applying the colours to the panel
with a metal spatula. This results in short,
scooped strokes of a thick impasto, allowing
greater modelling and depth of figures. The
girl came from a high-status family, as is
demonstrated by her jewels, which included
S-shaped hoop earrings with pearls, a thick
loop and a gold loop neck chain, and a large,
round, gold slide ornament with a central
red cabochon stone (normally a garnet or a

glass imitation during the Roman Period)
hanging from a long gold chain on her chest.
Only traces remain on the left shoulder.
Similar jewellery from excavated contexts
throughout the Roman world enables us to
date this panel to between the first and the
early second century AD.

PLASTER FUNERARY MASK

Gilded and painted plaster and linen, with glass inlays
Dimensions: 67,3 x 39 x 16,8 cm
Roman Period, mid 1st - early 2nd century AD
Provenance: Hawara, Faiyum, donated by Garré
Inv. no. S. 17134

In the Roman Period either a painted portrait panel or a plaster mask was placed over the mummies of persons of the wealthy class. The plaster masks were often highly elaborate, with inlaid eyes, and the medium allowed the artisan to mould jewels, draperies and contemporary hairstyles into the plaster. The present mask is entirely gilded, to stunning effect. A number of gilded masks were found at the site of Hawara, all datable to sometime between the mid first and early second century AD, and all have idealized features, often with inlaid glass eyes and eyebrows.

This bust-length mask commemorates a mature woman, whose hair is finely combed under a smooth veil that is decorated at the back with traditional Egyptian funerary imagery. Her drapery is loosely pleated and swirls around her breast, shoulder and upper arms. She is wearing a snake bracelet on each arm (the non-venomous *Elaphe longissima*, associated with the Greek god of healing Aesculapius), rings on her fingers, bird-shaped earrings (alluding to the sweet song of the Sirens), and a thick loop-and-loop chain with a pendant in the shape of a crescent moon, a fertility symbol. Her Graeco-Roman dress is a thin and close-fitting undergarment (*chiton*), and a thicker fringed mantle (*himation*), which is knotted at the chest. In her left hand she holds a large funerary garland, known throughout the ancient Mediterranean, an instance being those on figured limestone mausoleum capping stones at Palmyra. The gilding is significant in that the Egyptians associated gold with the skin colour of the gods, but on plaster masks of this type the metal was more liberally applied to the entire bust. The fact that the jewels are modelled on a plaster bust may also have been a way of economizing and frustrating the rapacious tomb robbers of antiquity.

MENSA ISIACA

Bronze inlaid with other metals
Dimensions: 74 x 123 x 7 cm
Roman Period, 1st century AD
Provenance: acquired in Rome from Pietro
Bembo in 1527, acquired by Charles
Emanuel I of Savoy in 1628, first displayed
in the Museo Egizio in 1832
Inv. no. C. 7155

From a 'romantic' point of view, one could
suggest that King Charles Felix of Savoy took
the decision to buy the Drovetti collection
in 1824, the core of the Museo Egizio, as
a result of the acquisition of the so-called
Mensa Isiaca some two centuries earlier
by King Charles Emanuel I. Indeed, this
enigmatic tablet was the reason why King
Charles Emanuel III had sent the botany
Professor Vitaliano Donati to Egypt in 1753
to acquire objects that might explain the
significance of this Egyptian-style temple
altar top, which first became known in
Rome in 1628.

The object is seemingly Egyptian in its
iconography, but does not in fact depict true
Egyptian rites. The attributes are mostly
invented, and the hieroglyphic inscriptions
framing the scenes are nonsensical. Despite
the bizarre attributes, the central figure
within a chapel is Isis. The altar was probably
made in Rome in the first century AD to
furnish a temple to Isis, possibly for the
Iseum Campensis, by an artisan and priests
who did not have a true understanding of
Egyptian religion. Nevertheless, the Isis cult
and its mysteries had a profound attraction
and exercised a great influence throughout
the Roman Mediterranean.

The images and texts are inlaid in the
bronze tablet in a variety of different metals
(refined silver, gold and copper alloyed
with a lot of gold), displaying advanced
metallurgical skills. For example, the black
metal used for certain details on the table,
usually incorrectly described as niello (silver
sulphide), is the product of alloying copper
and tin with small amounts of gold or silver
(about 2 %) and then 'pickling' it in organic
acid. The resulting black metal shapes were
then hammered into the cloisonné cells
of the table. Pliny (*Naturalis historia*) and
Plutarch (*Moralia*) both described this black
alloy as 'Corinthian bronze'.

SCALA

Photographs: Giacomo Lovera
Editing: Silvia Cosi
Page layout: Francesca Lunardi

Special thanks go to
Geoffrey Thorndike Martin,
Sara Caramello and Marco Rossani
for their invaluable assistance

ISBN: 978-88-8117-951-0

Printed by: Grafiche Flaminia, Foligno (Perugia)